CONFEDERATE IRONCLAD
VS
UNION IRONCLAD
Hampton Roads 1862

RON FIELD

First published in Great Britain in 2008 by Osprey Publishing,
Midland House, West Way, Botley, Oxford, OX2 0PH, UK
443 Park Avenue South, New York, NY 10016, USA

E-mail: info@ospreypublishing.com

A CIP catalog record for this book is available from the British Library

ISBN: 978 1 84603 232 5

Page layout by: Ken Vail Graphic Design, Cambridge, UK
Index by Alan Thatcher
Typeset in ITC Conduit and Adobe Garamond
Maps by Peter Bull Art Studio
Originated by PDQ Digital Media Solutions
Printed in China through Bookbuilders

08 09 10 11 12   10 9 8 7 6 5 4 3 2 1

FOR A CATALOG OF ALL BOOKS PUBLISHED BY OSPREY MILITARY AND
AVIATION PLEASE CONTACT:

NORTH AMERICA

Osprey Direct, c/o Random House Distribution Center, 400 Hahn Road, Westminster,
MD 21157

E-mail: uscustomerservice@ospreypublishing.com

ALL OTHER REGIONS

Osprey Direct, The Book Service Ltd, Distribution Centre, Colchester Road, Frating Green,
Colchester, Essex, CO7 7DW

E-mail: customerservice@ospreypublishing.com

Osprey Publishing is supporting the Woodland Trust, the UK's leading woodland
conservation charity, by funding the dedication of trees.

www.ospreypublishing.com

Artist's note

Readers may care to note that the original battlescene
paintings from which the color plates in this book were
prepared are available for private sale. All reproduction
copyright whatsoever is retained by the Publishers. All
inquiries should be addressed to:

H. Gerrard
11 Oaks Road
Tenterden
Kent
TN30 6RD

The Publishers regret that they can enter into no
correspondence upon this matter.

CONTENTS

INTRODUCTION

Ironclad oceangoing vessels were already in the process of revolutionizing war at sea when the American Civil War began in 1861. The main navies of the world had been experimenting with steam-powered propulsion and floating batteries for years before the advent of the Confederate casemated ironclad *Virginia* and the Union turreted ironclad *Monitor*. The earliest experiments in the use of iron plate to resist the force of cannonballs appear to have been made in France as early as 1810 by a "Monsieur de Montgery," an officer in the French Navy. Montgery proposed covering the sides of Napoleon's ships with several plates of iron of the aggregate thickness of 4 inches, but the French Emperor rejected the idea. Having lost the battles of the Nile and Trafalgar, Napoleon preferred to concentrate on his more successful land campaigns. In 1813, Pennsylvanian-born Robert Fulton designed the first US Navy (USN) vessel to use steam, which may be considered the prototype of the later steam-propelled ironclad. Although called the *Demologos* ("The word of the people") by its designer, the vessel was officially named the US Steam Battery *Fulton*. A catamaran-style hull with a centrally positioned paddle wheel, the *Fulton* was essentially a heavily armed and strongly-built "mobile fort" for coastal defense. Launched in late October 1814 while the War of 1812 was still in progress, she was completed shortly after Fulton's death in February 1815 and was delivered to the Navy in June 1816. However, old-fashioned Navy men could not imagine steam power replacing wind and sail. Her machinery was ignored, and she was rigged with sails. Apart from a single day of active service the following year when she carried President James Monroe on a cruise around New York Harbor, the *Fulton* was laid up until 1825, after which she served as a floating barracks at the Brooklyn Navy Yard and was finally destroyed when her magazine exploded on June 4, 1829.

Referred to as the father of the US steam navy, Commodore Matthew Perry commanded the second American steam frigate, also named USS *Fulton*, and commonly called *Fulton II*. A side-wheel steamer with three masts and two smokestacks, this vessel was launched at the Brooklyn Navy Yard on May 18, 1837, and was commissioned during the following December. She served along the Atlantic Coast, training officers in gunnery, conducting ordnance experiments, and aiding ships in distress. A major event in her early service occurred in November 1838 when she outmatched the British steamer *Great Western* in a speed contest off the New York coast. Decommissioned at New York on November 23, 1842, the *Fulton* was laid up until 1851 when she was redesigned with two masts and one smokestack, and given new engines and boilers. Continued service throughout the 1850s ended when she was grounded conducting antislave trading patrols off Cuba in 1859. Laid up at the Pensacola Navy Yard, Florida, she was still there in February 1861 when Florida authorities seized Federal facilities in the state. Though intended for service in the Confederate Navy, the *Fulton* was instead destroyed to prevent capture when Federal forces reoccupied Pensacola in May 1862.

In 1855 came the side-wheelers *Mississippi* and *Missouri*, the US Navy's first oceangoing steam-driven capital ships. Commissioned in 1841, the *Mississippi* served as the flagship of Commodore Perry during the Mexican War of 1846 through 1848 and during his voyage to Japan in 1851 to 1854. In later Civil War service, she destroyed the Confederate ram *Manassas* during Farragut's passage of Forts St Philip and Jackson at the mouth of the Mississippi River on April 24, 1862. She was finally sunk during operations against Port Hudson on March 14, 1863. The *Missouri* was commissioned early in 1842, and over the next year demonstrated steam propulsion

The close-range combat between the *Monitor* and *Virginia* on March 9, 1862, is captured perfectly in this engraving by J. W. Evans, based on an original drawing by Julian O. Davidson, published in *Battles & Leaders of the Civil War*. The damage to the smokestack, deck rails, and boat davits of the *Virginia*, much of which was caused during the action the previous day, is shown to good effect. The single stern gun port on the *Virginia* is inaccurate as the Confederate ironclad had three gun ports at bow and stern to accommodate her two pivot guns. (Author's collection)

technology in the Washington, DC, area, operating in the Gulf of Mexico. In August 1843, *Missouri* left the States to convey a US diplomat to Alexandria, Egypt. While at Gibraltar on August 26, 1843, she caught fire, exploded, and sank without loss of life. The remains of her sunken hulk were later demolished to clear the harbor.

The use of floating batteries reached the height of their popularity during the Crimean War. The chief proponent was Napoleon III, the French Emperor, who built three steam-powered floating batteries that were used to great effect against stone-built Russian fortifications in the allied attack on Kinburn in the Black Sea on October 17, 1855. Efforts by the US to build a floating battery for harbor defense actually predated French developments. In 1842, Congress had authorized construction of a "shot and shell proof" armored steamer by Edwin and Robert Stevens, which became known as the Stevens Battery. When experiments showed the iron plate could not withstand cannon shot, the government rejected the proposed battery, and in 1861 the Navy once again rejected it.

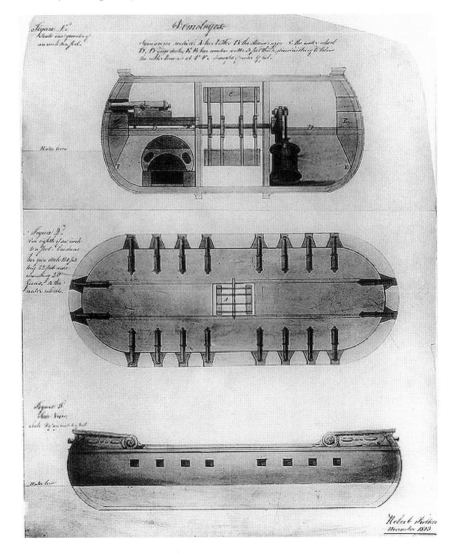

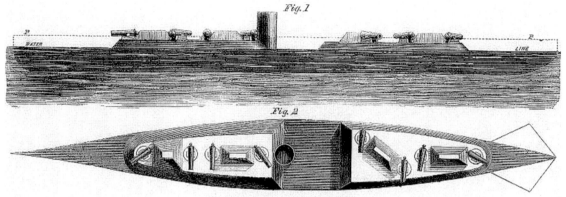

Fig. 1

Fig. 2

THE STEVENS FLOATING BATTERY.

Prior to the outbreak of the Civil War, the South began work on its first floating battery in January 1861 when John Randolph Hamilton, the son of a former South Carolina governor and commander of the short-lived South Carolina Navy, was ordered to build such a vessel "to assist in the reduction of Fort Sumter." One hundred feet long and 25 feet wide, the battery had two layers of railroad iron protecting its four large naval guns. Some men refused to serve on the unwieldy battery, nicknaming it the Slaughter Pen. General P. G. T. Beauregard ordered it to the Cove at the western end of Sullivan's Island, where it participated in the bombardment of Fort Sumter on April 12–13, 1861. The Confederates later broke up what became known as the Hamilton Floating Battery to use the iron plate in the construction of an ironclad.

Meanwhile, the French continued to modernize their navy and by August 1860 had launched *La Gloire*, the world's first truly ironclad warship, which was cased end-to-end with iron plates 4½ inches thick. The advent of this vessel was rapidly followed by the British HMS *Warrior*, which went into service in October 1861. US naval authorities had observed these developments but had not yet moved toward building their own ironclads when the Civil War began.

OPPOSITE:
The US Steam Battery *Fulton* had side-by-side twin hulls, as in Fulton's ferryboats, with the paddle wheel in the space between the hulls and protected by an upper deck with bulwarks and stanchions. This deck also sheltered the engine, which was in one hull, and the boiler, which was in the other. What Fulton had created was a catamaran. It was 150 feet long, 60 feet wide, and it had a slot, 14 feet wide, down its center. (Naval Historical Foundation photo NH 61883)

CHRONOLOGY

1861

April 20	Destruction of original USS *Merrimack* at Gosport Navy Yard
May 9	CSS *Atlanta* launched at Savannah, Georgia, but not completed and commissioned until nearly 16 months later
May 30	*Merrimack* salvaged by Confederates
August 8	Union Ironclad Board established
October 12	CSS *Manassas* becomes the first Confederate ironclad to attack a Union blockading ship
October 22	USS *Carondelet* (first *Cairo*-class river ironclad) launched

Photographed circa July 1862, Lieutenant William N. Jeffers, commanding the USS *Monitor* after the battle of Hampton Roads, is seated beside the gun turret in this photograph by James F. Gibson. Note the dent caused by a shell fired by the *Virginia*. (Naval Historical Foundation photo NH 48887)

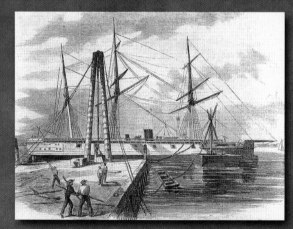

This engraving of USS *New Ironsides* being fitted out a Philadelphia, Pennsylvania, in mid-1862 was published in *Harper's Weekly* on August 23, 1862. This vessel joined the South Atlantic Blockading Squadron in January 1863. For the next year, she operated in support of the blockade of Charleston, South Carolina, and took part in several attacks on the Confederate fortifications defending that city. Her broadside battery of eight heavy guns on each side, coupled with her iron protection, made her a valuable ship for bombardment purposes during the Civil War. (Author's collection)

1862

January 30	USS *Monitor* launched
February 17	CSS *Virginia* launched and commissioned
February 25	*Monitor* commissioned
March 6	*Monitor* begins her voyage to Hampton Roads
March 8	*Virginia* attacks the blockading fleet in Hampton Roads
	Monitor arrives at Hampton Roads
March 9	CSS *Virginia* and USS *Monitor* clash in the battle of Hampton Roads
April 25	CSS *Arkansas* (first *Arkansas*-class ironclad) launched
May 6	CSS *Richmond* (first *Richmond*-class ironclad) launched
May 11	Destruction of the CSS *Virginia*

July 15	CSS *Arkansas* vs. USS *Carondelet* on Yazoo River
August 30	USS *Passaic* (first *Passaic*-class monitor) launched
December 30	Sinking of USS *Monitor* off Cape Hatteras, North Carolina, in a severe storm with the loss of four officers and 16 crewmen

1863

June 17	Capture of CSS *Atlanta* by USS *Weehawken* at Wassaw Sound
July 1	CSS *Albemarle* (first *Albemarle*-class ironclad) launched
July 29	Launch of USS *Onondaga*, the first twin-turreted monitor
August 1	USS *Canonicus* (first Canonicus-class monitor) launched

Best-suited for river combat the low freeboard and heavy turret of the *Monitor* made her highly unseaworthy in rough waters. As a result she foundered and sank while being towed south by USS *Rhode Island* during a heavy storm in the Atlantic off Cape Hatteras on December 31, 1862. Sixteen of 62 crewmen were lost in the storm. Based on descriptions by survivors, this engraving was published in *Harper's Weekly* on January 24, 1863. (Author's collection)

Prior to his appointment as commander of the *Monitor* on January 16, 1862, Lieutenant John Latimer Worden had become the first Confederate prisoner-of-war. Summoned to Washington early in 1861, he received orders in April to carry secret dispatches regarding the reinforcement of Fort Pickens south to the warships off Pensacola, on the Florida coast. Having delivered the dispatches, he was arrested near Montgomery, Alabama, during the return journey north and was held prisoner until exchanged about seven months later. Though still ill as a result of his imprisonment, Worden accepted orders to command the *Monitor* and reported to the construction site at Green Point where he supervised her completion. (Naval Historical Foundation photo NH 63712)

1864

March 10	CSS *Columbia* (first *Columbia*-class ironclad) launched
May 5	USS *Chimo* (first *Casco*-class monitor) launched
August 5	CSS *Tennessee II* v. USS *Chickasaw* in the battle of Mobile Bay

1865

January	Launch of CSS *Texas*, the last Confederate ironclad

DESIGN AND DEVELOPMENT

John M. Brooke was born at Tampa Bay, Florida, in 1826 and began his naval career as a midshipman in 1841, rising to the rank of lieutenant by 1861. After resignation from the US Navy in April 1861, he accepted a commission as a lieutenant in the CS Navy, and became involved in the construction of the *Virginia* and other Confederate ironclads. He also developed the Brooke rifled cannon, which was used in many of these vessels. (Naval Historical Foundation photo NH 58902)

THE *VIRGINIA*

In the first few months of the American Civil War, experimenting with warships naturally moved to the bottom of the list of priorities for the US Navy, as the North concentrated on the implementation of the blockade at sea and the overland campaign to bring the seceded Southern states to heel. By contrast, the newly formed Confederate States Navy (CSN) urgently required a means to overcome the vastly superior Union navy and looked to the developing technology of ironclads for a solution. Indeed, Confederate Secretary of the Navy Stephen Mallory stated, "I regard the possession of an iron-armed ship as a matter of the first necessity." If the Confederacy could build a viable ironclad warship before the North, they hoped that they could smash the Union blockade and impose their own blockade in its place. When the Union navy abandoned the Norfolk Navy Yard, in the Gosport suburb of Portsmouth, Virginia, on April 20, 1861, they scuttled 12 of the 13 vessels stationed or under construction there, including the steam frigate USS *Merrimack* (often misspelled as "Merrimac"), which, according to Confederate reports, was "burnt to the water's edge."

Meanwhile, Mallory continued his efforts to create an ironclad component to his tiny fleet and, to this end, met with Lieutenant John Mercer Brooke, CSN, on June 10, 1861. A career naval officer in the USN prior to the secession of Virginia, Brooke had developed a device for accurately mapping the deep seafloor while stationed at the Naval Observatory in Washington, DC. Also an ordnance specialist, he designed four of the guns for the battery aboard the *Virginia*, and later became Chief of the Confederate Navy's Bureau of Ordnance and Hydrography. Asked by Mallory to design "an ironclad war vessel," Brooke submitted rough drawings subsequently described as consisting of "a casemated vessel with submerged ends and inclined iron-plated sides. The ends of the vessel and the eaves of the casemate ... were to be submerged two feet; and a light bulwark or false bow was designed to divide the water and prevent it from banking up on the forward part of the shield with the vessel in motion, and also to serve as a tank to regulate the ship's draft."

Approving Brooke's design, Mallory ordered the master ship carpenter at the Norfolk Navy Yard to Richmond, the Confederacy's capital city, to aid in producing an accurate drawing and specifications. This individual made helpful recommendations regarding "details of timber," but was unable to produce drawings. Hence, about June 23 Naval Constructor John L. Porter and Chief Engineer William P. Williamson were also ordered from Norfolk to Richmond. A Virginian, Porter had recently resigned his post as Naval Constructor, the leading warship design post in the USN. When he arrived in Richmond, he had with him his own plans – plus a model for an "ironclad floating battery." These were similar to Brooke's plans in that they also consisted of an armored casemate with inclined iron-covered sides and ends, with guns mounted in broadsides, but the casemate was mounted on a simple hull without extended bow or stern. However, Porter's design was intended for a harbor defense vessel, while Brooke's plans were for a seagoing ship. Although Mallory considered Porter's idea, he elected to continue with Brooke's concept of a seaworthy ironclad that could not only defend Southern ports, but engage and destroy Union blockade ships.

Porter was subsequently given constructor's duties and ordered to prepare drawings based on Brooke's plan. Williamson became responsible for acquiring and installing the engines, while Brooke supervised the manufacture of the iron plate at the Tredegar Works in Richmond and the procurement of heavy rifled ordnance for the ship. In late June 1861, all three men went to the Gosport Navy Yard to search for engines strong enough to drive an ironclad. Finding none available, Brooke suggested salvaging the machinery from the wreck of the USS *Merrimack*. Though the frigate had been partially burned and sunk, her lower hull and power plant had been salvaged on May 30 under the supervision of Flag Officer Forrest French, Virginia Navy. Williamson suggested that it might be possible to use both the hull and engines of the *Merrimack* to build the new vessel. After further consultation, the three men agreed that converting the wrecked frigate to an ironclad was feasible at an approximate cost of $110,000 and brought the suggestion to Mallory, who approved the idea and issued

Photographed in 1907, John L. Porter was involved in converting the burned USS *Merrimack* into the CSS *Virginia*. He was born in 1813, the son of a shipwright at Portsmouth, Virginia, and became a Navy civilian employee in the 1840s. In 1859 he was appointed a naval constructor, but resigned from the US Navy in May 1861 to take up the same responsibility for the Confederate Navy. He continued to develop improvements in the basic casemated ironclad design throughout the war. (Naval Historical Foundation photo NH 47207)

USS *MERRIMACK*

Designed by Chief Naval Constructor John Lenthall in 1854, the USS *Merrimack* (often incorrectly spelled *Merrimac*) was the first of a new class of steam frigate in the US Navy to be driven by a screw propeller. Built and launched at Boston on June 15, 1855, and commissioned February 20, 1856, she was named for the river that flows south through New Hampshire and then eastward across northeastern Massachusetts before emptying in the Atlantic at Newburyport, Massachusetts. Also designed by Lenthall, her sister ships were the frigates *Wabash*, *Minnesota*, *Colorado,* and *Roanoke*. All five vessels were considered to be superior to any warship in the world when launched. A ship of 4,636 tons, the *Merrimack* was 275 feet from prow to stern, with a beam of 51 feet 4 inches and draft of 24 feet 3 inches. Considered a good sailing ship, her two horizontal, double piston rod, condensing engines made at the Cold Springs Foundry, New York, were designed for auxiliary use only. She was armed with 40 guns which consisted of 14 8in., 24 9in., and two 10in. smoothbore cannon. She had a complement of 519 men.

During initial trials along the East Coast, mechanical failures occurred that were to plague her whole career. On her fourth day out on a cruise from Norfolk to Havana in 1855, the *Merrimack's* propeller broke. Returning to Key West, she lost her rudder and had to be towed into harbor. She was subsequently towed back to Boston for repairs. Other defects noted by her crew included a tendency to roll heavily in the sea and the fact that her boilers overheated when under pressure.

Under Kentucky-born Garrett J. Pendergrast, she embarked on her maiden cruise to the Caribbean and

Western Europe in 1856 through 1857 visiting Southampton, Brest, Lisbon, and Toulon. Returning to Boston, she was decommissioned for repairs on April 22, 1857. Recommissioned on September 1, 1857, she was next assigned as flagship to the Pacific Squadron from 1857 until November 1859. Rounding Cape Horn, she conducted a cruise of the Pacific coast of South and Central America until ordered home on November 14, 1859. Upon returning to the Gosport Navy Yard at Norfolk, Virginia, on February 16, 1860, her engines were condemned, and the ship was put into ordinary for major refitting and repair. With the threat of secession looming in Virginia, Secretary of the Navy Gideon Welles became concerned for the safety of Federal vessels and property at the Gosport Navy Yard, and ordered Commander James Alden to Norfolk to take command of the *Merrimack* and remove her to the Philadelphia Navy Yard. Engineer in Chief B. F. Isherwood was also ordered there to repair the engines. Presented with difficulties by pro-Southern naval officers, who persuaded Commodore Charles S. McCauley, commanding the Navy Yard, not to allow *Merrimack* to escape, Alden abandoned his mission, and all but the hull of the vessel was destroyed by fire as Federal authorities abandoned Norfolk on April 20, 1861. (Author's collection)

orders for work to commence on July 11, 1862. Later that month, the Confederate Congress appropriated $170,000 to fund the project.

The work of transforming the *Merrimack* into the *Virginia* began by cutting her down to the old berth deck, which was within 3½ feet of her waterline. The lower half of the hull was then copper sheathed, and both the 29-foot-long bow and the fantail stern extending 66 feet, were covered over with 1-inch-thick iron plate. Both the bow and stern were to be awash once the ship was completed and in fighting trim. A casemate, or roof, of pitch pine and oak, 24 inches thick and inclining at an angle of 36 degrees, was erected along the 170 feet of the midship section of the hull. This

This lithograph of the *Merrimack* in dry dock at the Gosport Navy Yard being converted into an "iron battery" renamed *Virginia* was produced in 1906 by G. S. Richardson. (Naval Historical Foundation photo NH 58712)

extended from the waterline to a height over the gun deck of 7 feet. Both ends of this shielded roof structure were rounded so that pivot guns could be used as bow and stern chasers. An additional course of 1-inch-thick iron plate extended 3 feet from the deck to a depth of 3 feet below the waterline around the entire vessel. The lack of sufficient protection below the waterline, especially when the vessel was lightened through expenditure of shot and coal, was later to prove a major design weakness in battle on March 9, 1862.

Employed by the US government in the Gosport Navy Yard, and compelled to either "starve or to serve the Confederates" by "cutting down and fitting up" the *Merrimack,* a head workman named Mr Diggs recalled that "her roofing consisted first of 15-inch rafters, of 10-inch thickness, and lying close side by side. Across these, lying fore-and-aft, was a roofing of 5-inch pine plank. Next came four inches of oak plank, up and down. This made a roof of two feet thickness of solid wood, all firmly bolted and barred together – the whole being secured and steadied by strong iron braces and bolts, running crosswise as well as fore-and aft."

The iron plating that covered this wooden roof of the *Virginia* was manufactured at the Tredegar Iron Works, owned by Joseph Reed Anderson. Although Mallory wanted 3-inch-thick plating, none appears to have been available throughout the Confederacy. The original contract specified that the foundry at Tredegar roll 1-inch-

Based on inaccurate sketches supplied by "a mechanic" who came north under a flag of truce, this engraving of the *Virginia* published in *Harper's Weekly* on November 2, 1861, indicates the basic design of the vessel, but shows it sitting too high in the water and with the pilothouse aft of the smoke stack instead of at the bow. (Author's collection)

thick iron plates, but several tests conducted by Brooke at Jamestown Island, Virginia, indicated that armor of these dimensions would provide inadequate protection. Hence, work on the vessel was delayed while the Iron Works halted production in order to alter their machinery to accommodate the thicker metal. Eventually, a 2-inch-thick underlayer of iron plate measuring 8 feet long by 3½ feet wide was placed horizontally on the roof of the *Virginia*, while an outer layer of the same dimensions ran vertically to its pitch – the whole being 4 inches thick. This was bolted through the woodwork and riveted inside.

Thus armored, the ship was provided with a cast-iron, wedge-shaped ram weighing 1,500 pounds that projected 4 feet from her bow. Although ramming as a decisive offensive tactic had been virtually abandoned with the rise of large sailing ships mounting artillery toward the end of the medieval period, the advent of steam power had made this battlefield technique once again a viable strategy. Suggested as an afterthought by Stephen Mallory, who likened ramming to a "bayonet charge of infantry," the ram fitted aboard the *Virginia* was designed to protrude 3 feet from her prow. Bolted to the bow's stern head, and further secured by iron braces, it was unfortunately poorly mounted. While hammering the bolts that secured it to the vessel, a missed stroke by one of the local Gosport blacksmiths charged with its manufacture badly cracked one of the flanges holding it in place. Although it was apparent that the ram was improperly mounted, nothing was done to correct the problem. This weakness was also to have important consequences during the events of March 8–9, 1862, in Hampton Roads.

The pilothouse was forward of the single smokestack and was covered with the same thickness of iron as the sides of the ship. According to Master's Mate William A. Abbott, USN, who gathered information while imprisoned in Richmond, the helmsman aboard the *Virginia* peered through four separate grills shaped like "bull's eyes." The intervening space, or "spar deck," created on top of the casemate was grated with a 2 x 2-inch grille to provide ventilation to the gun deck. Access to the spar deck was provided by three grille hatchways with pivot shutter closures, one forward and one aft of the smokestack, and a third at midship. These were positioned directly over three hatches of similar construction in the gun deck, which facilitated the passage of ammunition, coal, and other supplies directly into the vessel. Lanterns were hung along the gun and orlop decks to provide lighting.

On February 15, 1862, Flag Officer French Forrest, commanding the Gosport Navy Yard, wrote to Porter regarding the possibility of placing "two small, light boats, hung at davits" on the sloping sides towards the stern of the *Virginia* to serve as lifeboats, should the vessel sink. These were in place before the vessel embarked on her maiden voyage into Hampton Roads.

The ten-gun battery aboard *Virginia* consisted of four single-banded Brooke rifled cannon, designed by ship designer John M. Brooke, and six 9in. Dahlgren smoothbores, two of which were converted to fire hot shot. Two of the Brooke rifles, one each at bow and stern on pivoting carriages, were 7in., of 14,500 pounds. These pieces were converted from 9in. Dahlgrens and were bored to 7 inches, and rifled and banded. The other two rifles were 6.4in. of 9,000 pounds, on two-wheeled Marsilly

carriages – one on each broadside abaft the smokestack. These guns were cast at the Tredegar Iron Works. Making up the remainder of the ship's broadside batteries, the 9in. Dahlgren smoothbores on Marsilly carriages were some of those captured at the Gosport Navy Yard. The Dahlgren gun had been developed for the USN by Rear Admiral John A. Dahlgren. Based on the shell gun invented by the French Admiral Henri-Joseph Paixhans in 1823, the improved American weapon was capable of firing round shot as well as shells. The two 9in. Dahlgren smoothbores forward of the smokestack were modified to fire hot shot heated in the boilers below. The ammunition taken onboard for the other cannon consisted of explosive shells and canister, which was effective against wooden ships, but would prove inadequate against another ironclad, which the *Virginia* faced on March 9, 1862.

Accommodation for the ship's complement of 320 officers and men appears to have been primitive. The officers were provided with temporary cabins below decks toward the bow and above the coal bunker, the partitions of which were taken down when the vessel was cleared for action. The men probably slung hammocks, or slept on the floor, along the gun or orlop decks. The ship's galley was aft of midship and located next to the magazine. According to Lieutenant Catesby ap R. Jones, Executive Officer of the *Virginia*, she was "badly ventilated, very uncomfortable, and very unhealthy." While the vessel remained at dock in Gosport, there was "an average of fifty or sixty [men] at the hospital, in addition to the sick list on board."

Once completed, the *Virginia* weighed 3,200 tons and measured 262 feet from bow to stern with a 51-foot 4-inch beam, and when fully armed sat about 21 feet deep in the water. As the cost of replacement was beyond the reach of the Confederacy, the condemned engines of the *Merrimack* provided the motive power for the converted vessel. These consisted of two horizontal, double piston rod, condensing engines fed by four boilers with 16 furnaces, which generated 1,200 horsepower and a speed of 9 knots. The steering chain mechanism was protected at the stern by an iron cover that was to prove ineffective in battle. The twin-bladed screw propeller was patterned on that designed by marine engineer Denis Griffiths and was the same type as that used on the British warship *Warrior*.

This more accurate wash drawing of the *Virginia* produced in 1898 by Clary Ray shows the pilothouse in the correct place at the bows, and superstructure in place, including metal frame work with canvas awning which could offer protection from the elements. (Courtesy of the US Navy Art Collection, Washington, DC)

CSS VIRGINIA

Key
1. Cast-iron ram measuring 4 feet in length and weighing 1,500 lbs
2. Bow-deck covered over with 1-inch thick iron plate with a rough-built wooden breakwater on top
3. Pilothouse with grills shaped like bull's eyes
4. Spar deck covered with iron grating
5. Chimney from stove
6. Iron hand rail
7. Ventilator
8. Smokestack
9. Wire braces for smokestack
10. Hatches with gratings and stairways
11. Powder magazine
12. Guns 6 through to 9: 9in. Dahlgren smoothbores on Marsilly carriages
13. Shell magazine
14. Dry provisions store
15. Lifeboat
16. Main staff flying Confederate ensign
17. Gun 10: Stern 7in. Brooke rifle on pivot carriage
18. Stern covered over with 1-inch thick iron plate
19. Iron chain cover
20. Steering chain mechanism
21. Rudder
22. Twin-bladed Griffiths pattern propeller
23. Copper-sheathed lower hull
24. One-inch thick iron plates extending 3 feet below waterline
25. Outer layer of 6-inch wide, 2-inch thick rolled iron plate (vertical)
26. Outer layer of 6-inch wide, 2-inch thick rolled iron plate (horizontal)
27. Propeller shaft
28. Bilge
29. Lower, or orlop, deck
30. Two horizontal back-acting engines, two cylinders, 72 inches in diameter, with 3-foot stroke
31. Guns 4 and 5: 6.4in. Brooke rifles on Marsilly carriages
32. Four Martin-type boilers with average steam pressure of 18 pounds
33. Coal bunker
34. Locations of temporary cabins for officers (partitions cleared for action)
35. Gun deck
36. Guns 2 and 3: 9in. Dahlgren smoothbores on Marsilly carriages, modified for hot shot
37. Elliptical gun ports, four to a side, and three to an end without any shutters
38. Gun 1: Bow 7in. Brooke rifle on pivot carriage
39. Anchor

Throughout summer 1861, Southern newspaper reporters as well as the general public visited the Gosport Navy Yard to observe the work on the *Merrimack*. As early as June 29, the Richmond *Daily Dispatch* reported that the vessel was being "fitted for service as a floating battery." The Reverend J. J. Nicholson was permitted aboard to view the ironclad in dry dock during August and reported to the Mobile *Tribune*, "I was on the celebrated Merrimac…. She is turned into a sort of terripin [sic], only with a sharper back…. Do you suppose a cannonball can have the courage to go through all that."

Not everyone believed the *Virginia* would be successful. In a private letter to a friend after the success of March 9, 1862, Chief Engineer Porter stated, "Hundreds – I may say thousands – asserted she would never float. Some said she would turn bottom side up; others said the crew would suffocate; but the *most wise* said the concussion and report of the guns would deafen the men. Some said she would not steer, and public opinion generally about here said she would never come out of dock." The North, however, took the Confederate ironclad more seriously. On October 6, 1861, Major General John E. Wool, commanding the Department of Virginia with headquarters at

Fort Monroe, advised Winfield Scott that the Confederate ironclad, still referred to as *Merrimack*, was being "constructed to resist cannon shot." On October 17, 1861, Flag Officer L. M. Goldsborough, commanding the Atlantic Blockading Squadron, reported that he had received "reliable information with regard to the preparation of the *Merrimack* for an attack on Newport News and these roads." He added that he felt "quite satisfied that unless her stability be compromised by her heavy top works of wood and iron, and her heavy weight of batteries, she will, in all probability, prove to be exceedingly formidable." A correspondent of the *New York Times* of October 28, 1861, reported from aboard the steamship *Atlantic* that "it had not been altogether unanticipated that the iron-clad Merrimac might at any moment round the sandy promontory and escape to sea.... I have heard grave fears expressed for the safety of the fleet as it lies at anchor here. Should the rebels be desperate enough for the undertaking, there is no doubt that a vessel such as the *Merrimac* is said to be could do immense injury to these unprotected transports. What could prevent her coming down some moonlight night and pouring a few broadsides of shells into our midst? The vessels are so numerous and close together that the havoc in such a case would be enormous."

THE *MONITOR*

As work proceeded on the *Virginia*, it became evident to the North that if the Confederacy succeeded in launching its vessel, there was not a Union ship that could stand up to her. Thus, the US Congress hastily made preparations to build its own ironclad. A board was established to investigate the possibility of completing the Stevens Battery, which still languished on the builders' stocks. Captain Charles Henry Davis, USN, was sent to inspect the vessel, but the report of the board was not published until the end of 1861, by which time other plans were afoot. In July an extra session of Congress had been declared by President Lincoln, and on August 3 legislation was approved to provide money for the construction of "one or more steel or iron-clad ships" for the Navy. The new law called for an examining board of three experienced naval officers to review the proposals and specifications that would be submitted in response to a printed public notice for such ships, which appeared in the press five days later. Vessels were to be "of sufficient capacity to carry an armament of one hundred and twenty tons, with a complement of three hundred men, and provisions for sixty days, with coal for eight days' steaming, and not to draw exceeding sixteen feet water." Applicants were advised that "Drawings of hull and machinery, with estimates of cost and speed, must be submitted." Those intending to apply had until August 15 to notify the Navy Department of their intentions, and plans and specifications were to be submitted with 25 days.

Established on August 8, 1861, the examining committee, known as the Ironclad Board, consisted of Commodore Joseph Smith, Commodore Hiram Paulding, and Commander Charles Davis. By September 16 these officers had examined proposals for at least 17 ships and recommended building three – the *Galena, New Ironsides,* and

Monitor. With convex, or "tumblehome," sides protected by interlocking iron bars, the *Galena* was designed by Samuel Pook for C. H. Bushnell and Company of New Haven, Connecticut, and would prove vulnerable to plunging fire at right angles when in action. Stripped of her ironcladding in 1863, she served the rest of the war as a wooden screw sloop. The *New Ironsides,* a casemated ironclad based on the French ship *Gloire* and proposed by Merrick and Sons of Philadelphia, provided successful Civil War service, but would be destroyed by fire in 1866. The first of a revolutionary class of ironclad battleship, the Ericsson Steam Battery, later in January 1862 named the *Monitor,* was a radical departure from conventional naval architecture. Although initially rejected as suitable only for inland waters, she was chosen for construction only after designer John Ericsson himself made a direct appeal and presentation to the Ironclad Board. At the same time, Lincoln backed the choice, stating, "All I have to say is what the girl said when she stuck her foot in the stocking. It strikes me there's something in it."

Swedish-born John Ericsson developed his engineering career from an early age. At age 13 he produced drawings for the Gota Canal and later served in the engineer corps of the Swedish Army from 1816 through 1826. Following a move to Britain, he formed a partnership with John Braithwaite and produced *Novelty,* one of the steam locomotive entries for the Rainhill Trials of 1829, an English competition in the early days of steam locomotion railways. Turning next to shipbuilding, he developed a successful screw propeller but, disappointed with the lack of support he received in Britain, migrated to the United States in 1839. With the backing of Captain Robert Stockton, a wealthy and influential naval officer from New Jersey, he designed and developed the USS *Princeton,* the USN's first metal-hulled, screw-propelled warship and the first to have its engines below the waterline. Unfortunately, a powerful 12in. gun called "the Peacemaker," devised by Stockton and forming part of the vessel's battery, exploded during a demonstration for President John Tyler in February 1844, killing six people, including Secretary of State Abel P. Upshur and Secretary of the Navy Thomas Gilmer. During the ensuing crisis, Stockton used his influence in the

The examining board appointed to select the revolutionary Northern ironclad vessel on August 8, 1861, consisted of Commodore Joseph Smith, Chief of the Bureau of Yards and Docks (left), Commodore Hiram Paulding, who was responsible for the evacuation of the Norfolk Navy Yard in April 1861 (center), and Commander Charles Davis, who would be promoted to Flag Officer commanding the Mississippi flotilla in May 1862 (right). According to Secretary of the Navy Gideon Welles, "All were officers of merit, but Commodore Smith, in addition to great nautical and civil experience possessed a singularly mechanical and practical mind. On him devolved, ultimately, the chief responsibility and supervision of the execution of the plans adopted." (Author's collection/Naval Historical Foundation photo NH 84379-KN/courtesy of the US Navy Art Collection)

Photographed looking forward along the port side shortly after her action with Confederate batteries at Drewry's Bluff, on the James River, Virginia, on May 15, 1862, the USS *Galena* was unsuccessful as an ironclad as her "tumblehome" sides were vulnerable to plunging shots. (Naval Historical Foundation photo NH 53984)

This engraving of USS *New Ironsides* being fitted out a Philadelphia, Pennsylvania, in mid-1862 was published in *Harper's Weekly* on August 23, 1862. This vessel joined the South Atlantic Blockading Squadron in January 1863. For the next year, she operated in support of the blockade of Charleston, South Carolina, and took part in several attacks on the Confederate fortifications defending that city. Her broadside battery of eight heavy guns on each side, coupled with her iron protection, made her a valuable ship for bombardment purposes during the Civil War. (Author's collection)

nation's capital to get the blame for the accident placed on Ericsson, whose name was anathema during much of the remainder of the antebellum period.

Thus, when Ericsson's ironclad design was finally accepted by the board in 1861, it faced opposition from many naval officers and the press, who were doubtful that a semi-submerged ironclad warship could float, let alone put to sea. Northern newspapers began printing reports about "Ericsson's Folly" and how this "cheese box on a raft" would slide to the bottom of New York City's East River upon launching. Ericsson himself was lamented as an "incapable schemer" and condemned for "the sin of wasting the resources of the country." Given the situation, Secretary of the Navy Gideon Welles hedged his bets and withheld 25 percent of the cost of the vessel until its captain had pronounced her a seaworthy and effective warship. Thus, when the *Monitor* steamed off toward her fateful encounter with the *Virginia* in March 1862, she was still partly owned by her builders.

In spite of contemporary criticism, work on the Ericsson "Steam Battery" went ahead with all haste. As US navy yards were not fully equipped to build ironclad warships in 1861, the hull of the vessel was built under contract with the private shipyard owned by the

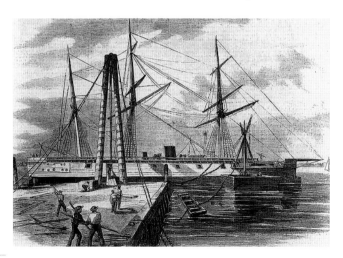

Continental Iron Works at Green Point, Long Island, New York. Fabrication of her engines was delegated to Delamater & Co., New York City, and the building of her turret was assigned to the Novelty Iron Works, also of New York City.

Construction began on October 25, 1861, and was completed in just 118 days at a cost of only $275,000. She was launched January 30 and commissioned February 25, 1862.

Central to the design of the vessel was a 120-ton revolving turret containing two smoothbore guns. Twenty feet in diameter and 9 feet high, the turret was formed of rolled 1-inch-thick iron plates bolted together to the thickness of 8 inches around an iron skeleton. When in its "stowed" position, the turret rested on a brass ring set in the deck. During battle stations, it was raised, or "keyed up." Integral to the forward side of the midships bulkhead was a Y-shaped structure called the turret support truss, which helped displace the weight of the turret resting on the deck above. In the center of the truss stood the turret shaft, which the crew raised into position by pulling a large wedge underneath. As a large nut was tightened on the end of the wedge, the shaft slowly rose up to connect with the yoke on the main beam at the bottom of the turret. Once the shaft was in place, a member of the gun crew turned a control wheel, which increased the steam pressure to the auxiliary steam engines and put the turret in motion. It took about 30 seconds to rotate it through 360 degrees.

Designed to house two XV-inch muzzle-loading Dahlgren smoothbores, only XI-inch pieces were available when the time came to mount the guns in the turret. Weighing nearly 9 tons each and firing solid shot weighing 140 pounds, these were mounted on specially designed "friction carriages" that brought the gun to a stop resting on the rear end of the chassis when fired. On recoil, the cannons cleared the carriage with only about 2 inches to spare. The elongated gun port openings were protected by thick iron port stoppers, or pendulums, that hung from the overhead. These were swung out of the way when the cannon was run out for firing and dropped

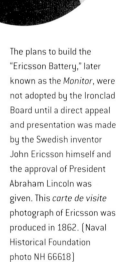

The plans to build the "Ericsson Battery," later known as the *Monitor*, were not adopted by the Ironclad Board until a direct appeal and presentation was made by the Swedish inventor John Ericsson himself and the approval of President Abraham Lincoln was given. This *carte de visite* photograph of Ericsson was produced in 1862. (Naval Historical Foundation photo NH 66618)

This contemporary engraving showing the launch of the USS *Monitor* at the Continental Iron Works at Green Point, New York, on January 30, 1862, is inaccurate as the turret was fitted after she was launched. (Monitor Collection, NOAA)

back into place on recoil to protect the gun crew from enemy fire. Because of the confined space inside the turret, each port stopper had a hole through its center to permit the handles of the gun tools to pass, allowing them to protrude outside the turret when the guns were being loaded. The loading implements hung from the overhead when not in use.

On January 27, 1862, Lieutenant John L. Worden, commanding the *Monitor*, reported to Secretary of the Navy Welles, "In estimating the number of her crew, I allowed 15 men and a quarter gunner for the two guns, 11 men for the powder division, and 1 for the wheel, which I deem ample for the efficient working of her guns in action. That would leave 12 men (including those available in the engineer's department) to supply deficiencies at the guns, caused by sickness or casualties."

A limited number of nonexploding solid shot, made at the Novelty Iron Works, was stowed along the base of the turret beside each of the guns. The turret floor had two hatches, one beside each gun, for access to the berth deck below. When the guns were in action, crew members would pass powder and exploding shells up to the turret. Two ladders in the turret led up to the roof, where the ship's officers gathered whenever the vessel was under way. The roof was covered with perforated plate that permitted smoke and fumes to escape when the guns were in action and a limited amount of fresh air at other times. To keep out rain and provide shade on hot days, the turret was fitted with an awning or canopy supported by a wooden center pole and stanchions around its edge. When under way and in foul weather, the crew removed the awning structure and battened down all the hatches. The only access to the outside of the vessel was from the turret roof via a removable iron ladder dangled over the side for the men to climb down to the deck.

Ericsson originally intended that the pilothouse, or wheelhouse, should be connected to the gun turret of the *Monitor*, but the exigencies of time and amount of work involved dictated otherwise. Thus the armored pilothouse was located toward the bows and accessed through a hatch in the floor. This structure was approximately 4 feet by 5 feet and rose 4 feet above the deck. It was constructed of iron "logs" measuring 9 by 12 inches thick that were bolted to oak beams below the deck, and ¼-inch gaps between the logs offered the only views out in all four directions. The

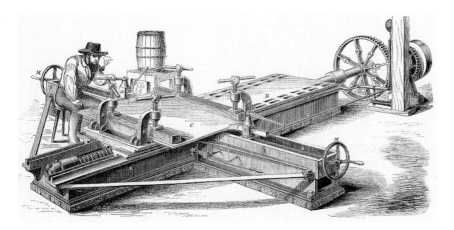

Armored plating for monitors was given a smooth finish by machines such as the Double Planer seen in the engraving published in the *Scientific American* on October 25, 1862. Invented by T. F. Rowland of Brooklyn, this machinery was kept busy building the Union ironclad fleet at the Continental Iron Works, New York, throughout the Civil War. (Author's collection)

cramped interior of the pilothouse measured only 45 by 35 inches, not including the area consumed by the ship's wheel, by means of which the quartermaster steered the vessel, while the pilot watched the waters. The captain also usually crowded into the pilothouse when the vessel was underway. Communication between the pilothouse and the gun turret was maintained via a speaking tube, which became disconnected early in the action on March 9, 1862. Badly damaged and restricting the view of the ship's guns during the battle of Hampton Roads, the pilothouse was lowered and modified by the addition of sloping sides. The navigation equipment used on the *Monitor* remains a mystery. A historical reference mentions "adjustments" to the ship's compass, but the iron mass of the vessel would have greatly affected such a small instrument.

The hull of the *Monitor* was constructed in two parts, with the upper section in the form of a flat-bottomed scow, with sharp ends and vertical sides, 5 feet deep, 174 feet long, and 41 feet 4 inches wide. The sides consisted of 30-inch-thick solid oak covered by 1-inch rolled iron plates to the thickness of 6 inches. The upper surface, or "deck," was protected by two layers of ½-inch-thick plates laid over the deck beams, which later proved vulnerable to plunging fire from fortifications.

The central portion of the bottom of the upper hull was cut out for a length of 124 feet and a width of 34 feet, to locate with the lower section, which was attached to the bottom of the scow and which extended down with inclined sides to a depth of 7 feet 6 inches. The lower section consisted of ½-inch-thick iron plates bolted together over a wooden frame. Fully fitted out, the vessel had a very shallow draft of only 10 feet 6 inches, and its deck reached barely 18 inches above waterline. The only permanent features seen above the deck were gun turret amidships and the armored pilothouse near the bow. Ericsson designed all other features of the ship, including smoke boxes, ventilator boxes, and bollards, to be removed prior to going into combat. Being under the projecting end of the upper section of the vessel, the screw propeller and rudder of the *Monitor* were securely protected from shot.

The lower deck of the *Monitor* was divided in two by a midship structural bulkhead, forward of which lay the berth deck, officers' quarters, magazine, and shell room. An open area beneath the turret measuring about 27 feet long by 18 feet wide,

The engine register of the *Monitor* was recovered from the wreck site off Cape Hatteras, North Carolina, in 2001 and is one of only two artifacts recovered from the wreck bearing the name of the vessel so far. Small metal disks seen in the six small apertures slowly clicked over to show the engineer how many hours the ship's engine had been working for. (Courtesy of The Mariners' Museum)

the berth deck offered sleeping space for the 48 enlisted men and a few of the unlucky junior officers that made up the crew. Although the Navy expected enlisted men to sleep in hammocks slung from poles inserted into sockets in the wooden deck overhead, most men preferred to spread their hammock on the wooden deck. The berth deck was crowded and provided little if any privacy. Ladders led up into the turret and onto the deck through the officer's hatch. All lighting on the berth deck was artificial, and the walls were painted white to help reflect the flickering glow of lanterns.

The powder magazine was situated on the starboard side of the berth deck, just forward of the midships bulkhead. Measuring 9 feet square, it was walled with iron and lined on the inside with lead to prevent any possibility of sparks. This provided storage for "loose" powder, cartridges, and exploding shells, which were held in specially designed copper tanks contoured to fit the shelves along the walls. A small number of "fixed" cartridges were kept filled and ready for use. To further prevent any chance of accidental explosion in the magazine, a "light room" was attached to the outside of the room, from which illumination from an oil lamp spilled into the magazine through a thick glass porthole. Also, the foyer-style entrance was secured with a heavy iron door. When left ajar during action, a thick canvas curtain covered the doorway. In case of fire below decks, the magazine could be flooded by opening a sea cock. The iron-walled shell room was located on the port side opposite the magazine. This held exploding projectiles, fuses, and cannon primers. Nonexploding cannonballs lay at the center of the berth deck, ready to be hoisted up to the guns, as well as in racks in the turret. A wooden bulkhead with a door in the center separated the officers' quarters and wardroom from the berth deck. The officers took their meals and socialized in the wardroom, where furnishings included an oak table, hardwood chairs, lanterns, and shelves. Blowers at the stern of the vessel

Key

No.	Item	No.	Item	No.	Item
1.	Rudder	13.	Captain's cabin (state room on starboard side)	25.	Berth deck (crews quarters)
2.	Propeller well and hatch			26.	Deck beams supports and bracings
3.	Ventilator	14.	Deck plating	27.	Main bulkhead
4.	Blower engine (on both sides)	15.	Boatswain's locker and storage (both sides)	28.	11-in. Dahlgren smoothbores
5.	Coal bunker bulkheads	16.	Anchor	29.	Main turret beam
6.	Turret hatch (one of two)	17.	Hand-powdered windlass	30.	Hull armor
7.	Turret frame stanchions (2.5 inches)	18.	Observation slit	31.	Boiler (one of two)
8.	Gun carriage rails	19.	Ship's wheel	32.	Engine bulkheads
9.	Turret support beams	20.	Pilot house	33.	Condenser (starboard side only)
10.	Turret traverse mechanism	21.	Tiller actuating ropes	34.	Engine
11.	Store rooms	22.	Officers' cabins	35.	Steam discharge pipes and stop valves
12.	Glass deck lights (covered when cleared for action)	23.	Wardroom		
		24.	Timber deck beams		

USS MONITOR

25

ventilated both the berth deck and the wardroom through perforated floor beams, while a radiator heated by the ship's boilers warmed the area in cold weather. Berthing for eight officers with four on either side lay to the outboard sides of the wardroom. The four cabins lining the wardroom were 6 feet long by 4 feet wide, while the other four were almost twice as wide, although the rising sides of the hull took up the added width. These were well furnished with black walnut berth, drawers, and closet. The captain's cabin and stateroom lay forward of the wardroom. Located on the starboard side, the cabin was 16 feet square and similarly furnished, with the added luxury of having its own flushing head. Of the same dimensions, the captain's stateroom was across a narrow passageway from the captain's cabin. Here the captain entertained important visitors and conducted day-to-day business. The boatswain's locker and storage were located either side of the captain's quarters. A passageway between the captain's rooms led to the chain locker in the bows of the ship. The anchor hoisting mechanism hung in the overhead, just forward of the ladder leading up to the pilothouse. Located below deck, the anchor could be raised or lowered at will without exposing crew members to the elements or enemy fire.

The area aft of the midship bulkhead contained the machinery of the vessel, plus the ship's galley and remaining heads. Two large, oval iron hatchways provided access to this area. When closed, these hatches created an airtight seal necessary to maintain the draft to the boilers provided by the belt-driven blowers in the engine room. The fire risk in this part of the ship was great, so the builders installed diamond-patterned, cast-iron floor plates throughout the engineering and galley areas. The first area aft of the bulkhead was the ship's galley. A large iron stove backed on to the boilers, while racks and shelves held cookware and utensils. The galley also held the "water closets." Two below-waterline flushing heads were situated on the starboard side for the enlisted men, while a single head for the officers was located on the port side. The *Monitor* was one of the first vessels credited with utilizing below-waterline flushing toilets, the operation of which took some getting used to. On one occasion, the ship's surgeon operated the valves in the wrong order and was propelled off his seat by a jet of water. Behind the galley stove stood the ship's two Martin boilers. Designed and patented in 1856 by D. B. Martin, Engineer-in-Chief of the US Navy, they measured 14 by 9 feet and provided the steam necessary to operate all of the ship's various engines and pumps. The screw was turned by two "vibrating side-lever" engines designed by Ericsson himself. Many ships' engines of the time had pistons that operated in a vertical motion, which occupied a lot of space and made them vulnerable to enemy fire because they were partially above the waterline. By contrast, the 30-ton, 400-horsepower engines aboard Ericsson's vessel had pistons that moved horizontally, which reduced their height and allowed them to be mounted below the waterline and behind the ship's protective armor. A "rock shaft" lay on each side of these engines, which was connected to the piston trunk by a short arm. At the aft end of the rock shafts, arms were attached to the propeller shaft via connecting rods. As the pistons slid back and forth, the rocking motion translated into rotation at the screw shaft. The engine itself stood on a raised platform accessed via a set of stairs on the starboard side. From this area, the engineering crew had access to all moving

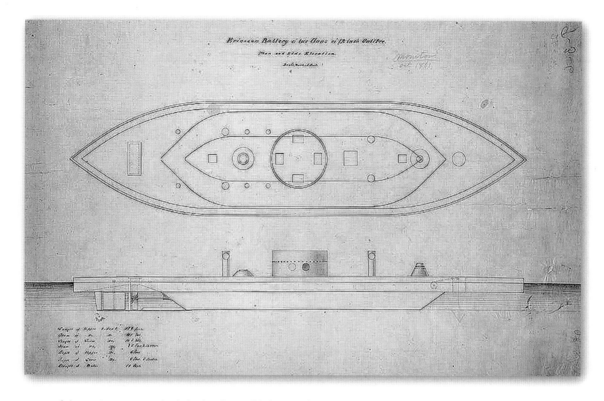

parts of the main engine, which had to be well lubricated. At the back of the engine was the valve chest, which was the operational center for the main machinery. Using a series of levers, cranks, and wheels, crewmen worked the vibrating side-lever engine at the behest of the captain.

Two of the vessel's bilge pumps, capable of removing 2,500 gallons per minute, were located behind the valve chest. Ericsson also equipped the ship with a centrifugal Worthington bilge pump that could remove 3,500 gallons per minute. The air blower drive pumps providing ventilation were mounted floor-to-ceiling at the outboard sides of the fire room. The small steam engines drove the large blowers with thick leather belts.

The rest of the port and starboard sides aft of the boilers were partitioned for the ship's coal bunkers. A narrow passageway about 2 feet wide led between the boilers and the coal bunkers. In heavy seas, crew members had to be sure-footed when negotiating this walkway, as one misplaced step could land them against the side of a scalding hot boiler.

Conditions below deck were generally deplorable during the summer months when temperatures neared 100°F in the berthing areas, even with the vessel anchored in the shade. During June and July, temperatures in the galley could reach 130°F on an almost daily basis, while in the engine room they approached an unbearable 150°F. Indeed, Paymaster William Frederick Keeler found service in the South Atlantic Blockading Squadron aboard the gunboat USS *Florida* in 1863 "very pleasant, roomy and comfortable" compared with being "cabined, cribbed, and confined" aboard the *Monitor*.

This drawing shows the deck plan and side elevation of the USS *Monitor* as produced by John Ericsson in 1862. (US National Archives 783889)

WHEEL HOUSE

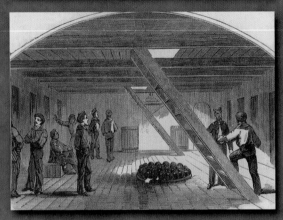

Based on a series of sketches produced by Theodore R. Davis, these engravings showing the interior of the *Monitor* were published in *Harper's Weekly* on April 12, 1862. Although partly inaccurate, they were approved by the ship's officers, and offer a valuable insight of life aboard the vessel. **(1)** A much over-sized view of the interior of the pilothouse with quartermaster at the ship's wheel and an officer standing by. Note the viewing slits and speaking tubes at right, which malfunctioned during the battle of Hampton Roads. **(2)** Supposedly looking fore and aft, this view of the berth deck features the ladders giving access to the turret and solid shot stored in the center of the deck. **(3)** Located immediately aft of the midship structural bulkhead, the ship's galley is seen with oval iron hatchways at right and turret shaft mechanism overhead. This view is inaccurate as the stove should have been shown backing on to the ship's boilers at left. **(4)** The captain's cabin was lined and furnished with black walnut and elegantly furnished with table and chairs. **(5)** The wardroom provided a communal area for the officers, with doors either side leading to their cabins. **(6)** The engineer officer and assistants tending one of the two Martin boilers and vibrating side-lever engines. (Author's collection)

TECHNICAL SPECIFICATIONS

Both the *Virginia* and *Monitor* were revoltionary vessels in terms of armor and guns. With less access to resources, the Confederacy utilized and adapted what she could, while the Union took advantage of its industrial might in order to produce the most advanced warship in the world at that time.

CSS *VIRGINIA*

Dimensions: Length, 262 ft 9 in; Beam, 51 ft 2 in; Draft, 20 ft 10 in. forward, 21ft 6 in. aft

Designed speed: 8.89 knots

Launch: February 1862

Cost: $170,000

Rate: Original type of casemated ram

Tonnage: 3,200

Engines: Two horizontal, double piston rod, condensing engines made at the Cold Springs Foundry, New York

Boilers: Four Martin-type with average steam pressure of 18 lb

Armament: Four single-banded Brooke rifles and six 9in. Dahlgren shell guns

Crew Size: 320

USS *MONITOR*

Dimensions: Length, 173 ft; Beam, 41 ft 4 in; Draft, 10 ft 4 in.

Designed speed: 7 knots

Acquisition: Built by contract with John Ericsson at Green Point, Long Island

Launch: January 30, 1862

Cost: $275,000–$280,000

Class: Monitor; screw steamer; iron and wood; single turret Rate: Original type of turreted vessel

Tonnage: 987

Engines: Double trunk, cylinders (2-in-1 casting); 36-in. diameter, 27-in. stroke

Boilers: Two; return tube "box" boilers

Armament: Two XI-inch Dahlgren guns in turret

Crew size: 63

PROJECTILES

By the beginning of the Civil War, bigger naval guns and coastal artillery were loaded with "semifixed" ammunition as well as solid shot. The former consisted of an explosive shell that was hollow and filled with a powder charge ignited by a time fuse. This projectile was attached via copper straps to a sabot, or wooden disk about the same diameter as the shell, which prevented an accidental discharge inside the barrel by keeping the fuse pointed outward toward the muzzle of the gun. The sabot could also be used with round shot to prevent it from rolling on the deck of the ship. Iron rings were attached to the top of the metal straps for attachment to a hoisting sling to facilitate loading.

Solid shot, or spherical balls, could skip across the water and strike an enemy vessel at the waterline, causing severe damage. Wadding continued to be used with this type of projectile after sabots came into use and could be made of almost any suitable material at hand, although straw or hay was most common. The hay was first twisted into a 1-inch rope, then a length of the rope was folded together several times and finally rolled up into a short cylinder, a little larger than the bore.

The time fuse caused the shell to explode at just about the point of impact by adjusting its length to the time of flight of the projectile. Some shells had three time fuses that, depending on the distance to the target, could be set to detonate the powder charge at 3½ seconds, 5 seconds, or 7 seconds after firing. Good artillerists generally succeeded in having their shells explode almost at the instant of striking. Other systems used percussion fuses employing a plunger-and-anvil mechanism that detonated the shell on impact and concussion fuses that were designed to activate from the shock of the projectile striking an object. A specially designed naval fuse employed a crooked channel so that the flame would travel faster than the water, enabling the shell to explode once submersed. Originally covered with a lead pull tab, this was removed before firing.

Guns also fired canister filled with about 48 iron or steel balls in a metal container and held firmly in place with a matrix of sawdust or similar material. Upon firing, the cylinder burst, spraying the balls in the manner of a giant shotgun blast. This was attached to a wooden sabot with four tacks that guided the projectile through the bore of the gun.

The *Virginia* entered battle on March 9, 1862, totally unprepared to engage another ironclad ship. She had only explosive shells (both spherical and conical), hot shot and canister to use against wooden vessels. Charged with arming and equipping the ship's battery, the choice not to carry armor-penetrating bolts for the Brooke rifles would haunt executive officer Lieutenant Catesby ap Roger Jones. In 1912, Chief Engineer Ashton Ramsay wrote, "If we had known we were to meet her [the *Monitor*], we would have at least been supplied with solid shot for our rifled cannons." In his memoirs, Eugenius A. Jack, who served aboard the *Virginia* as Acting Third Assistant Engineer, reinforced this point when he wrote, "Our only hope to penetrate the *Monitor's* shield was in the rifled cannon, but as the only projectiles for those were percussion shells, there was barely a chance that we might penetrate our adversary's defense by a lucky shot."

Guns aboard CSS Virginia

Type	9in. Dahlgren smoothbore x 6	6.4in. Brooke rifle x 2	7in. Brooke rifle x 2
Material	iron	double-banded (d/b) iron	d/b iron
Weight of tube, lbs	9,000	10,675	15,300
Length of bore, inches	107.3	117	121
Type of projectile	hot shot, case shot, canister	case shot, canister	case shot, canister
Weight of projectile, lbs	72.5	95	110
Weight of charge, lbs	10	8–10	10–13
Range, yards	1,170	2,200*	7,000*

*Estimated from the range of other rifled cannon

Guns aboard USS *Monitor*

Type	XI-in. Dahlgren smoothbore x 2
Material	iron
Weight of tube	15,700 lb
Range	3,400 yd

Projectiles

	CSS *Virginia*	USS *Monitor*
Hot shot		
Weight	about 90 lb	–
Diameter	8.8 in.	–
Case shot or spherical shell		
Weight	about 26 lb 4 oz with sabot	–
Weight of shot	–	about 168 lb
Weight of charge	–	15 lb
Diameter	about 6.25 in.	10.8 in.
Sabot	wooden	wooden
Straps	copper	copper
Conical shell		
Weight	about 110 lb	–
Diameter	6.9 in	–
Length	16.75 in.	–
Sabot	lead	–
Solid Shot		
Weight	–	187 lb
Diameter	–	10.8 in.
Canister with spherical ball		
Weight	about 30 lb	about 30 lb
Diameter	6.25 in.	10.8 in.
Length	8 in.	14.in.
Contents	–	48 iron balls packed with sawdust
Sabot	wood	wood

ENGAGING THE ENEMY

The two 6.4-inch Brookes rifles aft of the smoke-stack aboard the *Virginia* were designed by Lieutenant John Mercer Brooke. Similar in appearance to Parrott guns, the method of reinforcement of the breech was different. Whereas an iron band was welded to the tube of a Parrott in one piece, Brooke heated several heavy wrought-iron rings. When expanded, they were placed tightly around the breech. Once the iron cooled, it contracted over the breech, and forged a very strong band. The reinforced breech, created by the shrinkage hoops around the barrel, provided the metal with resilience to the internal force of exploding powder. The Brooke gun tubes were mounted on wooden Marsilly carriages. First used by the French navy, they were noted by John Muller, professor of fortifications and artillery at Woolwich, in his *Treatise of Artillery* published in 1757. The Marsilly carriage was adopted by the US navy and employed with all IX-inch shell guns in broadside. This type of carriage reduced recoil and was more easily traversed, or pointed, than guns on an ordinary truck carriage.

LOADING AND FIRING A 6.4-INCH BROOK RIFLE

"Serve Vent & Sponge!"

The gun captain (1) seals the vent with his thumb stool, or gloved thumb, while the sponger (3) and loader (4) swab out the barrel with a dampened sponge. The sponger (3) stands ready with a pre-measured, colour-coded cartridge he has received from the powder man (17). The shell man (7) opens the shell-box, disengages the shell and makes it ready to pass to the sponger.

"Load!"

The sponger (3) places the cartridge in the muzzle and pushes it into the bore. The loader (4) places the rammer into the muzzle, and pushes the cartridge steadily to the bottom of the bore. As the loader withdraws the rammer, the sponger receives the shell and places it, sabot first, into the muzzle, and removes its cap, which is passed along to the gun captain. The sponger then pushes the shell into the bore. The loader enters the rammer and gently but firmly pushes in the shell. Meanwhile, the handspike man (2) places the roller handspike under the rear transom of the carriage, and two teams of five men (7, 9, 11, 13, 15 and 8, 10, 12, 14, 16) take hold of left and right hand breeching ropes respectively. The gun captain (1) checks that vent is clear and that the cartridge has been rammed home properly.

In the case of hot shot, which was fired by Guns No. 2 & 3 aboard *Virginia*, i.e. the two Dahlgren guns commanded by Lieutenant Eggleston forward of the smokestack, the shot was hoisted from below in an iron bucket, placed by means of slings and a pulley in the muzzle of the gun. The muzzle was slightly elevated to allow the shot to roll against a well-soaked wad that rested against the powder. Another soaked wad kept the shot in place until the piece was fired.

"Run Out!"

The handspike man (2) heaves up on the roller handspike. The sponger (3) and loader (4) remove the truck-quoins, or wheel wedges. The five-man teams (7, 9, 11, 13, 15, and 8, 10, 12, 14, 16) heave on the breeching ropes. Once the gun is out, the handspike man swivels the roller handspike for training the gun, or removes it altogether if the handspike alone is preferred. Side-tackle teams close up; rear man coils end of the breeching rope to clear it from recoil.

"Prime!"

The second gun captain (2) pricks the cartridge bag by ramming a wire pricker through the vent-hole. The gun captain (1) inserts a priming tube into the vent, and attaches a lanyard to it. Meanwhile, handspike men (9 and 10) place themselves at the rear of the bracket

On the orders of ordnance inventor Captain John Dahlgren, solid shot was not used by the *Monitor*, as it was deemed "too heavy to fire with safety." According to an article in *The Scientific American* published on April 12, 1862, "The guns of the *Monitor* might have withstood the pressure in firing the solid wrought-iron shot, but discretion dictated a safe practice, for had a gun burst in the turret of the *Monitor*, she

SPONGE-LOAD

READY — FIRE

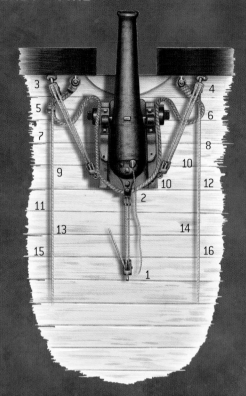

conveniently to heave forward or aft with handspikes.

"Point!"

The gun captain (1) adjusts the sliding-bar of the rear sight to proper distance given by the Officer of Division, and falls back so as to be clear of the recoil, lanyard in hand, face to the gun port, standing directly in the rear of the gun, with his eye ranging over the sights, and keeping in view the water-line of the opposing ship, trains the gun by voice or sign. A gun captain's assistant (6) throws back the hammer on the primer, and takes hold of the lever of the elevating screw. At the command "Right" or "Left," the side-tackle teams (3, 5, 7, 11, 13, 15 or 4, 6, 8, 12, 14, 16) haul on the breeching ropes , and the handspike men heave correspondingly on handspikes. The gun captain's

assistant elevates or depresses the elevating screw as directed.

"Ready — Fire!"

When sure of his aim, the gun captain (1) holds up a clenched fist and shouts "Ready" to signal to the officer commanding the gun division that the weapon is ready to fire. All the gun crew stand well back from the gun, and wait for the order to fire. Following approval from the division officer, the gun captain pulls the lanyard firmly. Instantly with the explosion, the gun recoils as far as its breeching ropes permit. The sponger and loader (3 and 4) place the truck-quoins in front of the wheels. The gun captain (1) puts back the hammer on the primer and coils up lanyard, and the exercise is ready to repeat.

would have become the trophy of the *Merrimac*." Furthermore, the Union guns were fired using the standard explosive charge of 15 pounds specified by the 1860 ordnance instructions for "distant," "near," and "ordinary" firing, and established for the USN by Dahlgren himself. Had double charges of 30 pounds been used, the *Monitor* may have destroyed the *Virginia,* especially at close range.

THE COMBATANTS

CSS *VIRGINIA*

The executive officer of the CSS *Virginia* was Franklin "Old Buck" Buchanan, who commanded the James River Fleet with the rank of Flag Officer. A Marylander, he had resigned his commission in the USN in April 1861, but when his native state failed to secede, he attempted to withdraw his resignation. Rebuffed by the Navy Department, which dismissed him from the service during the following month, he joined the CSN, receiving a captain's commission in September 1861. After heading the CSN's Office of Orders and Detail, Buchanan was placed in command of the defenses of the James River, Virginia, and used the Confederate ironclad *Virginia* as his flagship. Wounded in the action on March 8, 1862, he was forced to leave the ship before the clash with the USS *Monitor* the next day.

First Lieutenant Catesby ap Roger Jones was appointed by Virginia to the USN as a midshipman in 1836. He served under his uncle, Commodore Thomas ap Catesby Jones, during his voyage of exploration in 1848, rising to the rank of lieutenant. Appointed to the Navy Yard at Washington, DC, he assisted John Dahlgren with his ordnance experiments. Jones also took part in the maiden voyage of the USS *Merrimack* in 1856 as ordnance officer in charge of testing her Dahlgren guns. He tendered his resignation from the USN on April 17, 1861, and was commissioned lieutenant in the CSN on June 11 of the same year. He was initially placed in command of the defenses on Jamestown

Island, Virginia, and was assigned as executive officer of the *Virginia* on November 11, 1861. Selection of the ship's battery and arming and equipping of its marines was left entirely to him. As a result of Buchanan's wounds on March 8, 1862, Jones commanded the Confederate ironclad during her duel with the *Monitor* and continued to serve aboard *Virginia* until her destruction in May 1862.

First Lieutenant John Taylor Wood was a grandson of Mexican War hero General Zachary Taylor and began his nautical career as a midshipman in the USN on April 7, 1847. He served aboard the USS *Cumberland* and was teaching gunnery tactics at the US Naval Academy at Annapolis, Maryland, when the Civil War began. Resigning his commission on April 2, 1861, he was appointed as an officer in the CSN by October and assigned to the *Virginia* on November 25, 1861. He commanded the stern pivot gun on March 8–9, 1862.

Born in Washington, DC, First Lieutenant Hunter Davidson also served in the USN until April 1861, when he resigned and accepted a commission as first lieutenant in the CSN during April 1861. He was assigned to the North Carolina Squadron until transferred to the CSS *Patrick Henry*, following which he was detailed to the *Virginia* on December 8, 1861. He commanded the first division and guns No. 2 and 3 during the battle of Hampton Roads. He later invented the spar torpedo and would command the Confederate Submarine Battery Service, which was responsible for mine warfare in the James River. First Lieutenant Robert Dabney Minor served as Flag Lieutenant, or adjutant, to the executive officer aboard *Virginia* and was taken ashore having been wounded during the action of March 8. The other ship's officers consisted of First Lieutenants Charles C. Simms, John R. Eggleston, and Walter R. Butt. The ship's surgeon was Dr Dinwiddie B. Phillips who was assisted by Algernon S. Garnett. Lieutenant Douglas F. Forrest, CS Army, son of Commodore French Forrest, commanding Norfolk Naval Yard, was aboard as a volunteer "Naval Aide de Camp" in Buchanan's quarters on March 8, 1862. Serving as Acting Chief Engineer, Lieutenant Henry A. Ramsay was aided by Assistant Engineers Marshall Jordan, John W. Tynan, Loudon Campbell, Benjamin Herring, Eugenius A. Jack, and Elsberry V. White.

The crew of the *Virginia,* numbering 320 men, were hard to obtain. Of these, only 75 originally enlisted in the CSN. Referred to as "a sprinkling of old man-of-war's men" by Lieutenant Eggleston, these veterans of the USN and merchant marine included a paymaster's clerk, ship's corporal, boatswain's mate, captain of forecastle, captain of top, gunner's mate, quarter gunner, yeoman, carpenter and carpenter's mate, officer's cook, officer's steward, four quartermasters, captain of the hold, eight firemen, 24 seamen, seven coal heavers, and seven landsmen. According to Virginius Newton, a midshipman aboard the steamer CSS *Beaufort*, some of these were secured after "the defeat and dispersion of our gunboats at Roanoke Island." Others were acquired via recruiting stations, called naval rendezvous, established at Norfolk, New Orleans, and Richmond. The remaining crew members were made up, according to Eggleston, "mostly of volunteers from the various regiments stationed about Norfolk

Photographed after promotion to the rank of commander in April 1863, Catesby ap Roger Jones had served as ordnance officer on the steam frigate *Merrimack* when she began active service in 1856. Resigning his US Navy commission in 1861, he joined the short-lived Virginia Navy and soon became a Lieutenant in the CS Navy. When Captain Buchanan was wounded during the attack on USS *Cumberland* and *Congress*, Jones took command of the *Virginia*. (Naval Historical Foundation photo NH 48723)

at the time." Newton recalled that they proved to be "as gallant and trusty a body of men as any one would wish to command; but what a contrast they made to a crew of trained jack tars!"

The Confederate Army resisted attempts by the CSN to recruit from its ranks. Commanding Confederate forces on the Peninsula, General John Bankhead Magruder made it very difficult for Lieutenant Wood to collect men in late January 1862 by switching some of those with experience as mariners or artillerymen for those he considered to be of "a very different class." Most men were acquired from Virginia units with the United Artillery of Norfolk, Co. E, 41st Virginia Infantry, under Captain Thomas Kevill, providing 31 volunteers. Sixteen of these men manned a IX-inch broadside gun while the others were used to fill in on the other guns. Although their gun had its muzzle shot off during the engagement with the *Cumberland*, they continued to serve their piece throughout the clash with *Monitor* the next day. Others from Virginia included 21 men from the 9th Virginia Infantry, stationed at Craney Island, at the entrance of the Elizabeth River, looking out across Hampton Roads. The next largest contribution came from North Carolina and Louisiana units, with 20 men offering their services from the 1st North Carolina and 12 men from the 15th Louisiana. One man from Coppens' C. S. Zouave Battalion, from Louisiana, also volunteered. Others came from Alabama, Arkansas, Georgia, South Carolina, Texas, Mississippi, and Maryland.

Eggleston recollected that the *Virginia* had "a crew that had never even seen a great gun like … they were soon to handle in a battle against the greatest of odds ever before successfully encountered." He also stated that "the first and only practice of these men behind the guns of the *Merrimac* herself was in actual battle." In fact, the gun crews of the *Virginia* were trained aboard the decrepit frigate USS *United States* for about two weeks prior to leaving dock on March 8, 1862.

The 54-strong CS Marine Guard aboard *Virginia* consisted of two sergeants, two corporals, one musician, and 49 privates, and was commanded by Virginian and Mexican War veteran Captain Reuben Thom. Sergeants Jacob S. Scholls of Pennsylvania and Joshua Charlesworth of Maryland were both veterans of the US Marine Corps. Most of the other ranks were enlisted in the cities of New Orleans,

Memphis, and Mobile. A detachment of marines manned one of the guns aboard the *Virginia*, while the others served as riflemen, targeting the gun ports and viewing slits of the pilothouse aboard *Monitor*.

USS *MONITOR*

On March 6, 1862, the USS *Monitor* left New York with a crew of 63 consisting of – 12 officers and 51 seamen. The men who served aboard the vessel would develop a special bond with each other during the nine months they spent together, and they soon came to refer to themselves as "Monitor Boys." Born in New York, Lieutenant John Latimer Worden had served 28 years in the USN when he was appointed to command *Monitor*. During the battle with *Virginia* on March 9, he received facial wounds that partially blinded him when a Confederate shell exploded just outside the pilothouse. Worden relinquished control to his second-in-command and the vessel's executive officer, Marylander Samuel Dana Greene, son of General George Sears Greene, a future hero of the battle of Gettysburg. Greene commanded the twin Dahlgrens in the gun turret during the battle on March 9, 1862.

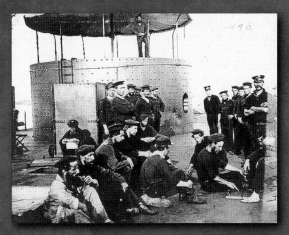

Photographed in July 1862, crew members of the *Monitor* gather on deck by a smoke box aft of the gun turret. Seated at bottom left is 39-year-old Gunner's Mate Joseph Crown. Born in New York City, Crown enlisted for a three-year term on January 20, 1862. He was transferred from the receiving ship *North Carolina* to the *Monitor* three days before the duel with the *Virginia* and served aboard the Union vessel until December 31, 1862, following which he was transferred to the monitor *Catskill* for the remainder of the war. Standing with arms folded left of center is Coal Heaver William Durst, who was transferred to the *Monitor* on February 25, 1862. Records show that he deserted on November 6, 1862, but reenlisted on February 16, 1863, under the alias Walter David. He served on other vessels until May 31, 1864. Seated immediately beneath Durst is 23-year-old Michael Mooney. Born in Ireland, he worked as a grocery store clerk in New York City when the Civil War began. Enlisting in Co. H, 12th Regiment New York Volunteers, he served in the infantry until September 1861. On February 14, 1862, he enlisted in the navy for a three-year term as a coal heaver, and 11 days later was transferred to the *Monitor*. He was promoted to Second-Class Fireman on November 7, 1862. Surviving the loss of the *Monitor*, he served as Second-Class Fireman on the *Catskill* until August 2, 1863, and then on the screw frigate *Wabash* until November 30, 1863. He was discharged at Brooklyn, New York, on December 28, 1863. Standing at far right is 30-year-old Robert Williams. Born in Wales, he enlisted in New York for a three-year term as a First-Class Fireman on February 15, 1862. He went down with the *Monitor* on December 31, 1862. (Naval Historical Foundation photo NH 574)

Chief Engineer Alban C. Stimers had served as chief engineer aboard the *Merrimack*, and was on the board evaluating the completion of the long-overdue Stevens Battery. Beginning in November 1861, he superintended construction of the *Monitor* and accompanied the vessel to Hampton Roads as an observer. Though not officially assigned to the Federal ironclad, he performed many of the chief engineer's duties, until Isaac Newton and his assistant engineers got used to their task. (Naval Historical Foundation photo NH 44389)

From Massachusetts, Louis N. Stodder was appointed acting master the day after Christmas 1861 and was assigned to the receiving ship *Ohio*, from where he was given orders to join the *Monitor*. He was stationed at the wheel that operated the revolving the turret on March 9 and was seriously injured when a shell from the *Virginia* struck that part of the vessel. Acting Master Joshua N. Webber had charge of the powder division on the berth deck. As no pilot was available, Worden accepted the volunteer services of Acting Master Samuel P. Howard. Doing duty aboard the frigate *Minnesota*, he was an important acquisition the night before the battle, as his knowledge of the ground in and about the Hampton Roads was invaluable.

An assistant to Ericsson, Chief Engineer Alban C. Stimers was aboard to observe the performance of the *Monitor*. Another New Yorker, he entered the USN as a third assistant engineer in January 1849. Though not formally a member of the ship's complement, he took part in her difficult voyage from New York to Hampton Roads and offered advice to the ship's engineers. During the historic battle on March 9, he manned the wheel controlling the revolving turret of the *Monitor* after Lieutenant Stodder had been wounded at that post.

An experienced steamboat captain and engineer, First Assistant Engineer Isaac Newton Jr. passed orders to Second Assistant Engineer Albert B. Campbell, who actually operated the ship's machinery. The Third and Fourth Assistant Engineers were Robinson W. Hands and Swedish-born Mark T. Sunstrom. William Flye was also aboard as an acting volunteer lieutenant. Other officers aboard the *Monitor* included Acting Assistant Surgeon Daniel S. Logue and Acting Assistant Paymaster William F. Keeler, who oversaw all accounts, pay books, and provisions.

The crew aboard the *Monitor* was comprised of three-year volunteers whom Worden had selected from the receiving ship *North Carolina* and ship of the line *Sabine*, two ships in the Brooklyn Navy Yard. Most were in their twenties, with the oldest being 38 and the youngest 18. These included men of immigrant stock born in Ireland, Sweden, Norway, and Wales. Swedes were particularly attracted to the vessel due to the nationality of its designer. Apart from Third Assistant Engineer Sunstrom, Seamen Hans Anderson and Charles Peterson were stationed in the gun turret during the battle on March 9. Born in Norway, Seaman Peter Williams was serving as quartermaster steering the *Monitor* in the pilothouse when Captain Worden was wounded. On April 3, 1863, he received the Medal of Honor for keeping his hands on the ship's wheel during the confusion that followed. Welshman David Ellis enlisted at New York on February 14, 1862, for a three-year term as a coal heaver. By March 6, 1862, he was transferred to the *Monitor* from the receiving ship *North Carolina*. Two crew members were black and at least one was Jewish. Although most indicated "none" under "occupation" in the muster roll, a few listed "carpenter," "stone cutter," "chandler," or "machinist." One man listed as a "sail-maker" must

These officers aboard the *Monitor* were photographed on July 9, 1862 by Matthew Brady photographer James F. Gibson. *Standing, top row, left to right:* Master's Mate George Frederickson, Fourth Assistant Engineer Mark Trueman Sunstrom, Acting Assistant Paymaster William F. Keeler, and First Assistant Engineer Isaac Newton. *Seated in chairs, middle row, left to right:* Lieutenant Samuel Dana Greene, Acting Master Louis N. Stodder, Acting Master E. V. Gager, Acting Volunteer Lieutenant William Flye, and Acting Assistant Surgeon Daniel C. Logue. *Seated on deck in front, left to right:* Third Assistant Engineer Robinson W. Hands and Second Assistant Engineer Albert B. Campbell. (Courtesy of Steven F. Jamrisko)

undoubtedly have been otherwise employed aboard the *Monitor*. The vessel did not rate a Marine Guard hence there were no Marines aboard. However, Peter H. Brodie was entered as a "Drummer Boy" and his duties would have included beating the crew to quarters.

Approximately 18,000 African Americans served in the Union navy during the Civil War. Crouching at center in this domestic scene aboard the *Monitor* is Siah Carter. Rowing out to the vessel as a runaway slave while it was anchored off City Point, Virginia, on the night of May 15, 1862, he was considered "contraband of war" by the Union sailors and signed aboard the *Monitor* as a first-class ship's boy with duties as ship's carpenter and assistant cook. Carter served on the ironclad for seven months and survived the sinking on December 31, 1862. He remained in the Navy for the duration of the war and was honorably discharged from service on May 19, 1865. (Library of Congress LC-B815-660)

THE STRATEGIC SITUATION

When the Civil War began, President Lincoln met with his generals to devise a strategy by which the rebellious Southern States could be brought back into the Union. Major General Winfield Scott, the aged commander of the US Army since 1841, proposed a plan of campaign that became known as the Anaconda Plan. A native of Virginia, Scott believed that the majority of Southerners did not support secession and desired complete reunification with the United States. In order to restore the Union with as little bloodshed as possible, he favored a relatively nonaggressive policy involving a complete blockade of the South. Too old to command in the field, Scott advised Lincoln to adopt a plan consisting of a naval blockade of the Southern ports and a strong thrust down the Mississippi River valley. In so doing, he believed that Northern forces would isolate the Confederacy from outside help and "bring it to terms." Initially mocked by the Northern press as Scott's "boa constrictor" plan, it subsequently became more appropriately known as the Anaconda Plan, after the aquatic species of boa snake that squeezed its prey to death from a watery lair.

For the Anaconda Plan to succeed, it would be necessary to blockade more than 3,500 miles of coastline from Hampton Roads, off the coast of Virginia, to the Rio Grande River, on the border with Mexico, and up the Mississippi River from New Orleans to New Madrid Bend. Such a plan would take time to implement, as the USN would need to acquire more ships to make the blockade effective. Furthermore, gunboats would need to be built and men trained for the expedition down the Mississippi. As the proud Southern people would not be starved into submission overnight, patience was also an essential part of the Union strategy. This did not suit an impatient Northern press and public that demanded an

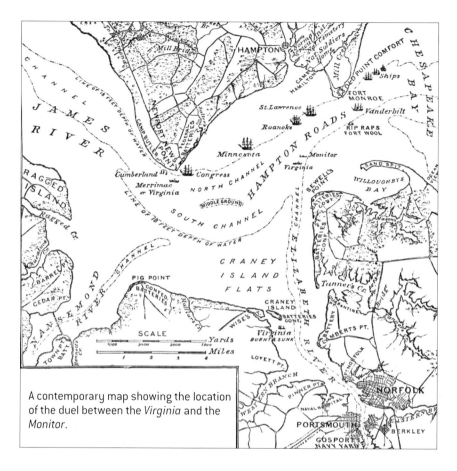

A contemporary map showing the location of the duel between the *Virginia* and the *Monitor*.

overland invasion from Washington, DC, in order to capture the Confederate capital at Richmond.

Lincoln ultimately adopted a modified version of Scott's plan in which a naval blockade remained central, but which included an overland advance into Virginia. To meet the challenge of forthcoming naval operations, Secretary Gideon Welles began a massive expansion of the US fleet. In spring 1861, the Navy consisted of 82 ships, which included the *Merrimack*-class frigates and *Lancaster*-class sloops. But by December of that year there would be 264 ships in the Navy, and by the end of the war, the Northern navy would maintain a force of 618 vessels. At the same time, a roster of 7,600 men in navy service in 1861 increased to over 51,000 by 1865.

For both the North and the South, one of the most strategically important coastal regions was Hampton Roads, where the James, Elizabeth, and Nansemond Rivers meet the Chesapeake Bay at the tip of the peninsula formed by the James and York Rivers. For the North, this was the doorway to the Confederate capital at Richmond, and General McClellan would choose this peninsula as his avenue to attack the Confederate capital. In so doing, he would have logistics and fire support from the rivers that run down both its sides. For the South, it was an outlet to the sea and potential European allies. Known as "the Gibraltar of the Chesapeake Bay," Fortress Monroe, the massive stone fort that guarded the inward approaches to the Roads, remained solidly in Union hands. It would become the jumping-off place for many Union expeditions into the South, as well as an anchor for the blockade of the Atlantic Coast. By the beginning of 1862, the Atlantic Blockading Squadron had five Union ships, mounting a total of 219 guns, guarding the mouth of the James River at Hampton Roads. These consisted of the two steam frigates *Minnesota* and *Roanoke*, and three wooden sailing ships, the *St. Lawrence, Congress,* and *Cumberland*. By March of that year, these ships were supported by over 55 other vessels, consisting of supply ships, transports, tenders, tugs, and dispatch vessels.

Meanwhile, the Confederacy pressed ahead with the construction of its revolutionary war ship, CSS *Virginia*. On February 17, 1862, she was launched and christened with little ceremony and, according to an eyewitness, with "only four marines and a corporal" aboard. She was commissioned three days later, but rode too high in the water due to the fact that Porter had forgotten to subtract the weight of the old frigate's masts, upper decks, sails, and rigging when calculating the ironclad's displacement. Even when powder, shot, and shell, plus 150 tons of coal were taken aboard, the vessel continued to sit high in the water, exposing too much of the thinner 1-inch iron plate that encased her hull to a depth of only 3 feet. This would continue to be serious design flaw that affected her performance on March 9, 1862.

Nonetheless, with this vessel nearing completion, Buchanan considered how best to use her. Much to the disappointment of Secretary of the Navy Mallory, who was hopeful that the *Virginia* would be seaworthy and capable of making either "a dashing cruise up the Potomac as far as Washington [D.C.]," or even attacking the Brooklyn Navy Yard in New York, she was difficult to turn, and with a draft of 22 feet, she was not suited to negotiate the maze of shallows and narrow channels of the Elizabeth River and Hampton Roads, let alone the Potomac River. Even with an experienced pilot, she would be unable to get close to either Fortress Monroe or Newport News. A large area of shallows between Sewell's Point and Pig Point limited her area of operations even further. Nor could she steam far up the James River toward Richmond. But she could be used to attack the vessels of the Union blockading squadron in Hampton Roads, and she was accordingly readied for that purpose.

On March 4, 1862, Buchanan wrote to Mallory from aboard "the Steam Frigate *Virginia*" outlining his plan of operation, stating, "On Thursday night the 6th instant, I contemplate leaving here to appear before the Enemy's Ships at Newport News." He also wrote to Commander Tucker of the James River Squadron, requesting him to stand by to assist. However, Lieutenant Jones did not think the *Virginia* was ready for action, and he advised delay. None of the shutters on the gun ports had been fitted, and powder and shot had only just been installed aboard the vessel. Departure was delayed for 24 hours, during which time Jones had the iron-plated sides of the *Virginia* covered with thick grease to "increase the tendency of projectiles to glance." He also had temporary shutters rigged at the bow and stern gun ports. All of the crew finally boarded the ironclad on March 6, and Jones reported that "all preparations were made."

Meanwhile, on the same day, the *Monitor* was towed out of the Brooklyn Navy Yard by the tug *Seth Low*. According to First Class Fireman John A. Driscoll, "not a whistle

Produced by marine artist Julian O. Davidson for the *Battles & Leaders of the Civil War* series published in 1887, this drawing depicts the CSS *Virginia*, accompanied by the tugs *Beaufort* and *Raleigh*, steaming passed the Confederate battery on Craney Island on her way to attack the Union fleet on March 8, 1862. (Author's collection)

sounded to cheer us as we went out. Those we passed seemed to think it would be better to have played the funeral dirge than to give us the customary cheer." In "clear, cold weather," she encountered calm waters outside New York harbor and steamed south accompanied by the *Seth Low* plus *Currituck* and *Sachem,* two wooden screw gunboats. Despite the lack of swell, Chief Engineer Stimers recorded that as soon as the vessel was outside Sandy Hook "the sea washed over the deck so deeply that it was not considered safe to permit the men to go on deck."

After a relatively uneventful passage past Long Beach and the Absecon lighthouse on the New Jersey coast, which lasted about 11 hours, the *Monitor* ran into heavy seas that by dawn of March 7 had developed into a full gale. With 10-foot-high waves breaking over it, the turret began to leak at its base. As originally envisaged by Ericsson, the turret was designed to rest on a brass ring, and its weight was considered sufficient to provide an effective seal. However, Worden had seen fit to ignore this recommendation and had attempted to make it more watertight by caulking it. This involved inserting oakum between the base of the turret and the ring. Under the pressure of the crashing waves, the oakum washed away and the sea poured through "like a waterfall." Also the berth deck hatch leaked, and the swell of the waves struck the pilothouse and rushed through the narrow eye slits with such force as to "knock the helmsman completely round from the wheel." Furthermore, the waves broke over the ventilation ducts and the water poured into the engine room in such quantities that it caused the blower belts to slip. Without adequate fresh air the engine room filled with carbon dioxide and carbonic gas. The lack of artificial draft caused the engines to stop due to a lack of air necessary for combustion. In turn, this caused the ship's mechanical pumps to fail. The *Monitor* was clearly not an oceangoing vessel as, indeed, Ericsson had stated at the outset of its construction. With the vessel filled with poisonous gases and beginning to sink, Worden signaled for help and the tug *Seth Low* towed her into the Delaware shore near Fenwick Island. In calmer waters, the engineers succeeded in venting the engine room and restarting the engines, including the main pumps.

With disaster averted, the *Monitor* resumed her progress south shortly after 8.00am on March 7, 1862. Lieutenant Greene reported a "smooth sea, clear sky … moon out, and the old tank going along five and six knots very nicely." About midnight, as she passed Chincoteague Island on the Maryland coast, the sea became rough again and started breaking over the smokestacks and ventilation ducts. With the engines struggling and the steering affected by loose tiller ropes, the vessel began to face broadside to the seas and rolled erratically. It seemed she might capsize at any moment. But by dawn of March 8 the tiller ropes were repaired and the seas had abated, enabling Worden to signal the *Seth Low* to tow the *Monitor* inshore again.

Having twice come close to disaster, the ironclad remained afloat with engines still in reasonable working order. With the vessel pumped dry and the crew revived with breakfast, the *Monitor* continued her voyage south under tow. Worden finally sighted Cape Charles at the northern entrance to Chesapeake Bay about noontime and was on the last leg of his perilous voyage. After one last setback when the towing hawser had to be reattached after parting, the Cape Henry lighthouse was in sight at about 4.00pm, and Worden spied black smoke lingering over Hampton Roads beyond. As his tiny flotilla steamed into the bay, he saw shells bursting in the air ahead. Clearly, the *Monitor* had arrived too late to save the blockading fleet from the *Virginia*. Worden finally ordered the anchor dropped in Hampton Roads alongside the flagship USS *Roanoke* at 9.00pm and received orders to protect the *Minnesota*. Steaming over toward the stricken frigate, he prepared his vessel and crew for the battle the next day.

In the meantime, at 11.00am on March 8, 1862, the *Virginia* had begun her journey down the Elizabeth River to Newport News as the tug CSS *Beaufort*, commanded by Lieutenant William H. Parker, nudged her away from the dock and then followed close behind with the tug *Raleigh* also in attendance. In contrast with that of her erstwhile foe, the *Monitor*, the departure of the *Virginia* received much attention. According to an eyewitness account published two days later in a local newspaper, the Norfolk *Day Book*, "It was a gallant sight to see the iron-clad Leviathan gliding noiselessly through the water, flying the red pennon of her commander at the fore flag-staff, and the gay Confederate ensign aft. Not the least impressive thought which she suggested, was that her gallant crew, under a commander and officers worthy to direct their destiny and defend the flag she bore, went thus with smiles and huzzas to solve a new problem in maritime warfare – to make the 'trial trip' of the Virginia the trial of battle."

It was 10 miles from the Gosport Navy Yard to Hampton Roads. With a top speed of about 6 knots under its own steam, and 7 knots with the river current, the ironclad took about 1½ hours to reach its destination. Buchanan summoned his crew to the gun deck toward the end of this period and, according to Acting Chief Engineer Ramsay, prepared them for battle, declaring, "Sailors, in a few minutes you will have the long-looked-for opportunity of showing your devotion to our cause. Remember that you are about to strike for your country and your homes. The Confederacy expects every man to do his duty. Beat to quarters."

The arrival of the *Virginia* at Hampton Roads at about 1.00pm caught the Union blockading fleet unprepared, with their "boats in the booms and wash clothes in the rigging." Engaging the 50-gun frigate USS *Congress* and the 24-gun frigate USS *Cumberland*, *Virginia* rammed the latter, losing her unstable ram in the process, and then forced the *Congress* aground off Newport News Point. At about 3.30pm the *Cumberland* sank. Approximately one hour later the *Congress* surrendered after taking heavy fire from the *Virginia*. Buchanan was wounded in the left thigh by a Minié ball during this action and was succeeded by Lieutenant Jones. Three Union steam frigates, the *St. Lawrence, Roanoke,* and *Minnesota,* ran aground while approaching the scene of battle from Old Point Comfort. The *Minnesota* was saved from possible destruction because the tide had ebbed, and the *Virginia* could not get close enough to her.

Observing from the beach at Newport News, Private Josh Lewis, 20th Indiana, recalled that the full broadside of the *Congress* "rattled on the armored *Merrimack* without the least injury." Commander William Smith of the *Congress* remembered that the Union shot bounced off the casemate of the Confederate vessel "like India-rubber balls." About 5.00pm the Confederate ironclad retired toward the mouth of the Elizabeth River with the intention of returning the next day to destroy the *Minnesota*. The next morning while returning from taking the dead and wounded ashore, Dr. Phillips, the ship's surgeon, ordered his boat to pull around the *Virginia* to observe the damage and recorded that he "found all her stanchions, iron railings, boat davits, and light work of every description swept away, her smoke-stack cut to pieces, two guns without muzzles, and ninety-eight indentations on her plating, showing where heavy solid shot had struck, but glanced off without doing any injury." He failed to notice that the "iron-shod beak" on her prow was also missing after ramming the *Cumberland*. The latter would be a major setback during her encounter with the *Monitor* the next day.

COMBAT

The day of the duel between the *Virginia* and *Monitor* dawned with fog lingering near Norfolk, Virginia. From the spar deck of the Confederate ironclad moored at the mouth of the Elizabeth River, Lieutenant Jones observed the *Minnesota* was still aground, and that an "iron battery," in all probability the *Monitor*, was close by her. Regardless of the fact that she was not supplied with the armor-penetrating bolts necessary to damage or sink another ironclad, he committed *Virginia* to battle. Shortly before 8.00am on March 9, 1862, the *Virginia*, accompanied by the gunboats *Patrick Henry, Jamestown,* and *Teaser,* slipped their moorings and got underway from Sewell's Point. Steaming in the direction of Fortress Monroe, they altered course after about ten minutes and headed toward the *Minnesota*, with the ironclad occasionally firing from its bow gun at the stricken frigate. Watching with Surgeon Daniel Logue, William Keeler, paymaster of the *Monitor*, recorded, "a shell howled over our heads and crashed into the side of the Minnesota… . We did not wait [for] a second invitation but ascended the tower & down the hatchway… . The iron hatch was closed over the opening & all access to us cut off."

Shortly before 8.30am Lieutenant Worden got his vessel underway, steaming toward the *Virginia* to meet and engage her as far away from the *Minnesota* as possible. Lieutenant Greene, executive officer aboard the *Monitor*, recorded, "Worden took his station in the pilot-house, and by his side were Howard, the pilot, and Peter Williams, quartermaster, who steered the vessel throughout the engagement. My place was in the turret, to work and fight the guns; with me were Stodder and Stimers and sixteen brawny men, eight to each gun. John Stocking, boatswain's mate, and Thomas Lochrane, seaman, were gun-captains. Newton and his assistants were in the engine and fire rooms, to manipulate the boilers and engines… . Webber had charge of the powder division on the berth-deck." As the speaking tube providing communication between the pilothouse

A map illustrating the major ironclad engagements of the war.

Map labels:

MISSOURI — St. Louis, Springfield
KENTUCKY — Louisville
VIRGINIA — Richmond ⊛ ①, Norfolk
NORTH CAROLINA — Wilmington
TENNESSEE — Nashville, Memphis
SOUTH CAROLINA — Charleston
OKLAHOMA
ARKANSAS — Little Rock
ALABAMA — Montgomery, Mobile
GEORGIA — Atlanta, Savannah ②
MISSISSIPPI — Vicksburg
TEXAS — Austin, Houston, San Antonio, Galveston
LOUISIANA — Shreveport, New Orleans ③
ATLANTIC OCEAN
Jacksonville
Gulf of Mexico
FLORIDA

1. Battle of Hampton Roads between CSS *Virginia* and USS *Monitor*, March 9, 1862
2. Action in Wassaw Sound, Georgia between CSS *Atlanta* and USS *Weehawken*, June 17, 1863
3. Action between CSS *Tennessee* and USS *Chickasaw* during the Battle of Mobile Bay, August 5, 1864

0 — 500 km
0 — 300 miles

and gun turret was broken early in the battle, Paymaster Keeler and captain's clerk Daniel Toffey, Worden's nephew, relayed orders and messages from the captain to Greene and his gun crews.

With the approach of the *Monitor*, the other Confederate gunboats withdrew from the battle, as the two revolutionary warships prepared to close with one another. Once the *Virginia* was within range, the *Monitor* opened fire at 8.45am, placing herself between the frigate and the ironclad. Aboard the *Virginia*, Acting Assistant Engineer Elsberry White recalled, "At this time we noticed a volume of smoke coming up from the opposite side of the *Minnesota* and there emerged the queerest looking craft afloat. Through our glasses we could see she was ironclad, sharp at both ends and appeared to be almost awash. Mounted amidships was a turret with ports and, as we looked, the turret began to revolve until her forward gun bore directly on us and, run out, it resembled a cheese box on a raft."

Observing the action from his river barge, Brigadier General Raleigh E. Colston, who commanded the Confederate defenses on the south side of the James River, stated, "No words can express the surprise with which we beheld this strange craft, whose appearance was tersely and graphically described by the exclamation of one of my oarsmen, 'A tin can on a shingle!' Yet this insignificant-looking object was at that moment the most powerful war-ship in the world."

Acting Assistant Engineer White continued, "We didn't have long to wait before she fired. Her first shot fell a little short and sent up a geyser of water that fell on our top and rolled off. We then fired our forward rifle and scored a direct hit on her turret, but with no apparent effect. Her next shot was better and caught us amidships with a resounding wham, but while the old boat shuddered, there seemed to be no

Entitled *The Ironclads,* this painting by the late Raymond Bayless shows the *Virginia* steaming resolutely towards the *Monitor* on March 9, 1862. The stricken frigate USS *Minnesota* is seen in the left middle distance. (Courtesy of the US Navy Art Collection, Washington, D.C. Donation of Raymond Bayless, 1975)

appreciable damage. By this time we were getting pretty close, and both crafts were firing as fast as the guns could be served. The men were stripped to the waist and were working like mad. Powder smoke filled the entire ship so that we could see but a short distance and its acrid fumes made breathing difficult."

Aboard the *Monitor,* Lieutenant Greene recorded that when the two vessels got within close range, Worden changed his course so as to come alongside the *Virginia.* He then stopped engines and passed the order, "Commence firing!" In response, the gun crews in the turret "triced up the port, ran out the gun, and, taking deliberate aim, pulled the lockstring." Of his experience in the gun turret, Greene recalled, "My only view of the world outside of the tower was over the muzzles of the guns, which cleared the ports by only a few inches. When the guns were run in, the port-holes were covered by heavy iron pendulums, pierced with small holes to allow the iron rammer and sponge handles to protrude while they were in use. To hoist these pendulums required the entire gun's crew and vastly increased the work inside the turret. The effect upon one shut up in a revolving drum is perplexing, and it is not a simple matter to keep the bearings. White marks had been placed upon the stationary deck immediately

A highly inaccurate lithograph by Kurz and Allison published circa 1889 combines both days of the battle of Hampton Roads by showing the USS *Cumberland* sinking and the *Monitor* engaged in combat with the *Virginia.* Commanding Camp Butler and the shore batteries lining Newport News Point, General Joseph K. Mansfield and staff stand in the foreground. (Library of Congress LC-USZC4-1752)

below the turret to indicate the direction of the starboard and port sides, and the bow and port sides, and the bow and stern; but these marks were obliterated early in the action. I would continually ask the captain, 'How does the *Merrimac* bear?' He replied, 'On the starboard-beam,' or 'On the port-quarter,' as the case might be. Then the difficulty was to determine the direction of the starboard-beam, or port-quarter, or any other bearing. It finally resulted, that when the gun was ready for firing, the turret would be started on its revolving journey in search of the target, and when found it was taken 'on the fly,' because the turret could not be accurately controlled."

The *Virginia* was quick to respond to Greene's guns, returning "a rattling broadside." According to Lieutenant Wood, who commanded the stern gun aboard the *Virginia*, his vessel delivered "a starboard broadside at short range, which was returned promptly... . Both vessels then turned and passed again still closer. The *Monitor* was firing every seven or eight minutes, and nearly every shot struck."

Despite suffering a hail of fire with every broadside received from the *Virginia*, the *Monitor* remained relatively undamaged. Greene recorded, "The turrets [sic] and other parts of the ship were heavily struck, but the shots did not penetrate; the tower was intact, and it continued to revolve." With relief, he added that "a look of confidence passed over the men's faces, and we believed the *Merrimack* would not repeat the work she had accomplished the day before." The lack of solid shot for the broadside guns, and absence of armor-penetrating iron bolts for the Brooke rifles, would account for the lack of penetration achieved by the guns of the *Virginia*.

Nonetheless, the crew of the Confederate ironclad fought on bravely. Painting a vivid picture of the scene below deck, Acting Chief Engineer Ramsay recalled, "On our gun-deck all was bustle, smoke, grimy figures, and stern commands, while down in the engine and boiler rooms the sixteen furnaces were belching out fire and smoke, and the firemen standing in front of them, like so many gladiators, tugged away with devil's-claw and slice-bar, inducing by their exertions more and more intense heat and combustion. The noise of the crackling, roaring fires, escaping steam, and the loud and

OVERLEAF
The Brooke 7-inch rifles at bow and stern of the *Virginia* were both mounted on pivot carriages which permitted them to fire at greater elevations and on a wider arc than those on the gun deck. In the confined space under the casemate, these guns were served by a reduced crew of 16 including the powder boy. The gun tube weighed 15,300 pounds, and fired round shot weighing 110 pounds to a maximum range of 2,200 yards.

Captured by the camera of James F. Gibson several months after its encounter with the *Virginia*, the turret of the *Monitor* bears the scars of battle. The modified pilot house with sloping sides is seen in the background, plus the deck lights with covers removed. Note the circular coal chute hatch set into the deck in the foreground, and cracked deck plates at lower right. The officers examining the turret are Lieutenants Albert B. Campbell, Second Assistant Engineer (left), and William Flyle, Acting Volunteer, USN (right). (Naval Historical Foundation photo NH 577)

labored pulsations of the engines, together with the roar of battle above and the thud and vibration of the huge masses of iron being hurled against us, altogether produced a scene and sound to be compared only with the poet's picture of the lower regions. And then an accident occurred that threatened our utter destruction. We stuck fast aground on a sandbar."

The 23-foot draught of the *Virginia* had confined her to a narrow channel of water, while the *Monitor* maneuvered more freely with her much shallower draught of 10 feet. In his after-battle report, Jones recorded, "The great length and draft of the ship rendered it exceedingly difficult to work her. We ran ashore about a mile from the frigate and were backing fifteen minutes before we got off." While the *Virginia* was stuck in the mud, the *Monitor* approached and fired several times at almost point-blank range. Phillips continued, "Taking a position very close to us, and where none of our guns could be brought to bear upon her, she directed a succession of shots at the same section of our vessel, and some of them striking close together, started the timbers and drove them perceptibly in, but not enough to do any serious damage."

In fact, the situation was critical for the *Virginia* at this stage. The coal consumption of the two days' battle had lightened her prow until her submerged deck was almost awash. The armor on her sides had been extended only about 3 feet below the waterline due to a hasty departure before completion. Lightened as she was, these exposed areas rendered her vulnerable. Had the *Monitor* depressed her guns and fired low along the waterline, she might have sunk the *Virginia* there and then. "Fearing that she might discover our vulnerable 'heel of Achilles,' while she had us 'in chancery,'" recalled Ramsay, "we had to take all chances. We lashed down the safety valves, heaped quick-burning combustibles into the already raging fires, and brought the boilers to a pressure that would have been unsafe under ordinary circumstances. The propeller churned the mud and water furiously, but the ship did not stir. We piled on oiled cotton waste, splints of wood, anything that would burn faster than coal. It seemed impossible the boilers could long stand the pressure we were crowding upon them. Just as we were beginning to despair there was a perceptible movement, and the *Merrimac* slowly dragged herself off the shoal by main strength. We were saved."

With his vessel again making way, and frustrated by the ineffectual fire of his vessel against the Union ironclad, Jones determined to ram the *Monitor*, unaware that he had lost his iron prow the day before. E. V. White recalled, "It was a last resort, seeing that our shots were ineffective, I was directed to convey to the engine room orders for every man to be at his post." It took about half an hour to maneuver the unwieldy *Virginia* into ramming position, while the *Monitor* continued to pound her. At one point, the executive officer was coming down the steps from the spar deck and observed a gun division standing "at ease," and enquired, "Why are you not firing, Mr. Eggleston?" The captain of the midship Brooke rifles replied, "Why, our powder is very precious, and after two hours' incessant firing I find that I can do her about as much damage by snapping my thumb at her every two minutes and a half." "Never mind," retorted Jones, "we are getting ready to ram her."

Finally, Jones issued the order, "Go ahead full speed," and the *Virginia* began her half-mile run steaming straight at the *Monitor*. Worden braced his vessel for the impact when he saw the Confederate ironclad begin its lumbering approach, fearing that his thin armored hull would be crushed by the weight of the larger ship. He relayed the message to the turret via Paymaster Keeler to "give them both guns." As he raced through the hull toward the gun turret, Keeler remembered thinking, "This was the critical moment, one that I feared from the beginning of the fight – if she could so easily pierce the heavy oak beams of the *Cumberland*, she surely could go through the ½-inch iron plates of our hull."

Just before striking the *Monitor*, Jones ordered his engines reversed too soon, which lessened the impact of the collision. Also, prior to being rammed, Worden instructed his helmsman to steer the more nimble Union vessel away to starboard, which caused the *Virginia* to affect only a glancing blow with its already damaged and leaking wooden prow. Of the moment of impact, Keeler recorded, "a heavy jar nearly throwing us from our feet – a rapid glance to detect the expected gush of water – she had failed to reach us below the water & we were safe." The only visual evidence of the ramming found after the battle was several wooden splinters from the hull of the *Virginia* stuck on a bolt head on the *Monitor*'s deck, plus a minor indentation in her iron plating.

In the gun turret of the *Monitor*, Greene fired solid 180-pound solid shot at point-blank range from both his Dahlgrens at the forward part of the casemate of the *Virginia*. "Had the guns been loaded with thirty pounds of powder, which was the charge subsequently used with similar guns," he commented later, "it is probable that this shot would have penetrated her armor; but the charge being limited to fifteen pounds, in accordance with peremptory orders to that effect from the Navy Department, the shot rebounded without doing any more damage than possibly to start some of the beams of her armor-backing."

According to Lieutenant Wood, "Both shots struck about half-way up the shield, abreast of the after pivot, and the impact forced the side bodily in two or three inches. All the crews of the after guns were knocked over by the concussion, and bled from the nose or ears. Another shot at the same place would have penetrated." While the *Monitor*

OVERLEAF
Unsuccessful in her attempt to ram the Union vessel, the *Virginia* shudders from the impact as shells from guns of the *Monitor* strike her stern during the battle of Hampton Roads. At the same time, the crew of the Confederate ironclad gather on the spar deck in a desperate attempt to board the *Monitor* as the two ironclads engage in close-quarter combat.

53

was momentarily alongside, Jones began to organize a boarding party to scramble aboard the deck of the Union ironclad and obscure the view of the commander by tying a canvas around the pilothouse. But the Monitor slipped astern before they could get on board. Meanwhile, Worden anticipated such an attempt and had ordered Greene to double-shot his guns with canister to repel boarders.

The battle continued with the exchange of further broadsides as fast as the guns could be served – and at very close range. By about 11.00am the supply of shot in the Monitor's turret was exhausted and with one of the two gun port stoppers jammed shut, she hauled off into shallow water for a short while to replenish and attempt a repair. The former involved hoisting 180-pound shot up in a sling from the berth deck while the turret remained stationary. The port stopper could not be repaired and remained jammed. Worden took advantage of the lull in battle and climbed through the porthole giving access to the deck outside the pilothouse to get a better view of his adversary. With ammunition replenished and one gun still operational, he renewed the contest.

Meanwhile, the Confederate ironclad had turned its attention once more to the Minnesota, firing several more shots that set the Union frigate ablaze again and destroyed the tugboat Dragon nearby. Soon after 11.30am, Worden decided to ram the Virginia in an attempt to damage the larger ironclad's vulnerable propeller and rudder, which was riding high in the water. According to Confederate Master-at-Arms William Norris, "Our rudder and propeller were wholly unprotected, and a slight blow from her stern would have disabled both and ended the fight." Steaming toward the fantail of the Virginia, the Monitor missed her target at the very last moment due to a malfunction in her steerage system.

As the Union vessel passed the stern of its opponent, Lieutenant Wood fired his 7in. Brooke gun at the Monitor's pilothouse. The shell struck the forward side of that structure directly on the sight hole, just as Worden was peering through the observation slit. The explosion cracked an iron log and created an opening in the top, while Worden received the full force of impact in the face, which temporarily blinded him. His injury was known only to those in the pilothouse and its immediate vicinity. Believing his steerage destroyed, Worden ordered Quartermaster Peter Williams put the helm to starboard and had the vessel withdrawn to assess the damage. He also summoned Lieutenant Greene to take over in the pilothouse while he was helped below, leaving Lieutenant Stimers as the only officer in the gun turret. Dazed and slightly concussed from the impact of shot and shell on the gun turret, Greene arrived on the scene and assisted in leading Worden to his cabin before taking command, for which he was afterward criticized by those who thought he should have immediately pressed on with the attack.

Meanwhile, Jones assessed the situation aboard the Virginia. Believing that the Monitor had given up the fight, and that he could not get any closer to the Minnesota, he passed along the gun deck, pausing at each division to hold an informal council of war with his lieutenants. It was agreed that, with the tide ebbing, the ship leaking at the prow, and the crew exhausted from being so long at their guns, the Virginia should return to Norfolk for repairs. Aboard the Monitor, Greene at last took his place in the pilothouse, only to find the Virginia steaming back in the direction of Sewell's Point. A few more shots were fired at about 12.15pm and the fight was over.

STATISTICS AND ANALYSIS

Crucial to understanding the outcome of the four-hour battle at Hampton Roads is the fact that the firepower of both the *Virginia* and *Monitor* was limited. The *Virginia* did not carry armor-penetrating bolts and had only a limited amount of solid shot for use as hot shot with two of her 9in. Dahlgrens. The gun crews aboard the *Monitor* were restricted by orders not to use solid shot or explosive charges over 15 pounds. Had double charges of 30 pounds been used, the *Monitor* may have destroyed the *Virginia* at close range, especially while she was stuck on the sand shoal. The US Navy Department subsequently issued orders that similar and larger guns aboard monitor-class vessels should in future use charges containing 30 pounds of powder. Hence neither ship was seriously damaged at Hampton Roads, and both sides were able to claim a victory. On March 10, 1862, the *Brooklyn Daily Eagle* declared, "The Merrimac disabled and the whole Rebel Fleet put back to Norfolk," while on the same day the *Richmond Daily Dispatch* announced a "Great Naval Victory" for the South.

Aboard the *Virginia*, several iron plates were cracked and the wooden frame of her casemate was forced back in several places, plus she had developed a new leak in her prow. The *Monitor* suffered damage to her pilothouse, dents in her turret, and several cracked deck plates. When the vessel came in for repairs at the Washington Navy Yard, Captain Dahlgren examined her and commented that he was "astonished to find that a man of her builder's cleverness had committed the error of exposing the flat surface of the turret to a direct blow instead of slanting its sides and thereby reducing the effect of a hit. His examination persuaded him that the vessel could not long stand the battering of an 11-inch gun. A 10-inch shot had done considerable internal damage, and four or five hits on the side had dished the armor considerably."

MONITOR GUN TURRET WITH XV-INCH GUN

Manual Exercise for working a XV-inch gun by Half-Crew.

"Serve vent and sponge!"

The gun captain (1) seals the vent with his gloved thumb. The sponger (3) passes to left of muzzle. The loader (5) passes the sponge-head and sections as required to the sponger, and assists in sponging. The gun captain then serves the vent with priming-wire and again closes it.

"Load!"

The shell man (13) receives the passing-box at the scuttle and passing a cartridge to the loader (5), who places it in muzzle. The loader then passes the rammer-head and sections to the sponger (3) and assists him to ram the cartridge home. The gun captain seals the vent, and four members of the gun team (9, 11, 13, and 15) hoist up the shell and offer it to muzzle. The sponger and loader (3 and 5) enter the shell in the muzzle. The loader removes the patch which is passed to the gun captain. The loader and sponger ram home the shell by sections as before.

"Prime!"/ "Elevate!" (or Depress)

The gun captain (1) seals vent and primes with powder from a flask or blank musket cartridge. He next turns the lever of elevating screw, sets the trunnion-sight at the proper degree of elevation and clamps it there. When the bubble of the trunnion-level is in the centre, he gives the order, "Well." The sponger and loader (3 and 5) then raise the muzzle by a section of rammer handle.

"Run out!"

Three members of the gun crew (7, 11, and 15) man the truck-crank to run out the gun. The compress man (9) eases the compressor. Three members of the gun crew (3, 5, and 13) man the gun port tackle. As the muzzle approaches, the port-stopper is raised at the command, "Open Port!" As soon as the gun is out, the truck man (11) un-ships the truck-crank and places it clear of the gun slide. The compress man turns the compressor-wheel with a rachet lever until hand taut. A crew member (15) turns the elevation lever and heaves well taut. The gun captain inserts the percussion-primer.

"Train right!" (or left).

The gun captain (1) sights through sight-hole, and orders "Right!" or "Left!" as the muzzle is to go. The Engineer at the starting-bar revolves the turret.

"Ready — Fire!"

When the target comes in view, the gun captain (1) gives order, "Ready – Fire." He then pulls the lock-string. The sponger (3) lets go port-tackle. The loader (5) closes the port. The engineer revolves the turret so as to point the gun abeam. This gets the scuttle clear for passing up more ammunition. Three members of the gun crew (7, 11 and 15) turn the crank and run the gun in. The compress man (9) eases the compressor with his lever. The gun is now ready for re-loading.

In terms of gunnery skills, the *Virginia* and *Monitor* were very well matched. According to the report of Chief Engineer Stimers to John Ericsson written immediately after the action, the *Virginia* struck the *Monitor* 22 times, hitting the "pilot house twice, turret 9 times, side armor 8 times, deck 3 times." Meanwhile, the Union vessel struck her adversary approximately 20 times out of 43 rounds fired during the battle. According to Eugenius Jack, "One shot struck directly over the outboard delivery. That was our weak spot. The shot broke the backers to the shield and sent a splinter into our engine room with about enough force to carry it halfway across the ship." In his recollections published in 1906, Acting Assistant Engineer E. V. White, who served on the gun deck in charge of the engine room bell and speaking tube during the battle, stated, "The balls from the *Merrimac*, especially those fired almost muzzle to muzzle, produced some results. Three cylindro-conical balls fired from the rifled guns made an indentation nearly four inches deep in the armor plating.

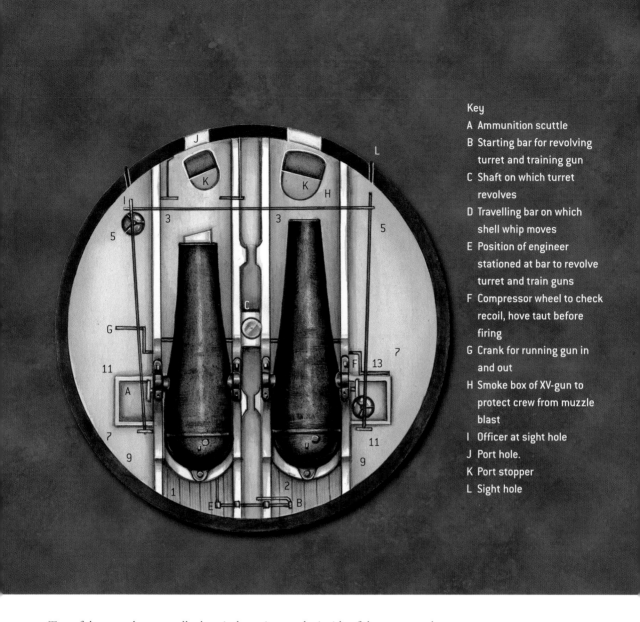

Two of them made an equally deep indentation on the inside of the turret, and a man leaning against the inside walls at the place receiving the blow was thrown forward and wounded…. The other shots which reached the *Monitor*, and were for the most part round, did not appear to me to have produced a very great effect, those especially which struck the sides perpendicularly; two, however, struck the side at the edge of the deck, lifting and tearing it, causing the iron plating to give way and breaking three of them. The others only produced insignificant effects."

Monitor designer John Ericsson opined that had the guns of his vessel been aimed lower, they would have sunk the *Virginia*. As it was, the projectiles glanced off the sloping sides of the Confederate ironclad instead of penetrating as they would if they had struck closer to water level. The Confederates were also surprised that the guns of the *Monitor* did not inflict greater damage to their vessel. Commanding the stern gun at Hampton Roads, Lieutenant Wood commented, "Not a single shot struck us

A damaged Dahlgren gun from CSS *Virginia* photographed at the Washington Navy Yard, DC, on April 27, 1933. Several other guns, relics of the Civil War and earlier conflicts, are seen beyond. The gun is inscribed, "One of the Guns of the Merrimac in the action with the U.S. Frigates Cumberland and Congress March 8th 1862 when the chase was shot off." The lower inscription reads, "The mutilation of Trunnions &c shows the ineffectual attempts to destroy the Gun, when the U.S. abandoned the Norfolk Navy Yard, April 20th 1861." (Naval Historical Foundation photo NH 1896)

at the water-line, where the ship was utterly unprotected, and where one would have been fatal."

Regarding casualties, the crew of the *Virginia* did not suffer significantly during the engagement with the *Monitor*, although two seamen were killed and three officers and five seamen were wounded during the action against the wooden ships and shore batteries on March 8, 1862. The crew of the *Monitor* suffered only three casualties during the battle of Hampton Roads. Lieutenant Worden lost his sight in one eye and was temporarily blinded in the other toward the end of the action. He would eventually recover sight in his right eye, but would remain permanently disfigured. Lieutenant Stodder and Seaman Peter Trescott were both temporarily concussed when a percussion shell from the *Virginia* hit the turret of the Union ironclad.

The lack of control of the revolving turret aboard the *Monitor* which, according to Lieutenant Greene, fired "on the fly," led to inaccurate gunnery by the Union gun crews. As William Norris, master-at-arms aboard the Confederate ironclad, noted, "The *Virginia* was so large a mark that almost every shot struck her somewhere; but they were scattered over the whole shield and on both sides, and were therefore harmless. To point her gun in our direction, and fire on the instant, without aim or motive, appeared to be the object. The turret revolving rapidly, the gun disappears only to repeat in five or six minutes the same hurried and necessarily aimless, unmeaning fire …"

A major drawback in the design of the *Monitor* was the positioning of the pilothouse toward the bow of the vessel. This meant the guns could not fire ahead or within several points of the bow, as the blast would have carried the structure away and killed its occupants. In fact, Ericsson originally designed the pilothouse to top the turret of the *Monitor*, but costs and limitations of time had precluded this. Based on a subsequent recommendation of engineer officer Isaac Newton, made immediately after the battle of March 9, 1862, a modified pilothouse of lower dimensions with sloping sides replaced the damaged original one. The height of the smokestack was also raised to prevent waves from dousing her engines.

FURTHER DEVELOPMENT

The battle of Hampton Roads received considerable international attention. On March 29, 1862, the London *Times* announced, "There is an end of wooden ships, and the Americans are now recognizing the fact to some purpose." Although they already had the *Warrior* and *Ironsides*, plus nine other ironclads under construction, the British hurriedly committed themselves to the further extension of their fleet of ironclad vessels. In France, the *(Paris) Constitutionnel* claimed that the Civil War in America would be remembered mainly for the clash between the *Virginia* and *Monitor*. In the Confederacy, the strength of coastal defense batteries was called into question. On March 11, 1862, Alfred L. Rives, the acting chief of the Engineer Bureau of the Confederate Army, advised, "The recent conflict at Newport News shows conclusively that water batteries, especially those near deep water, cannot injure materially properly constructed iron-clad vessels, nor contend with them."

The impact of the battle on naval thinking in the Union was summarized by Captain Levin M. Powell of the USS *Potomac* who later wrote, "The news of the fight between the *Monitor* and the *Merrimack* has created the most profound sensation amongst the professional men in the allied fleet here. They recognize the fact, as much by silence as words, that the face of naval warfare looks the other way now and the superb frigates and ships of the line ... supposed capable a month ago, to destroy anything afloat in half an hour ... are very much diminished in their proportions, and the confidence once reposed in them fully shaken in the presence of these astounding facts."

Although both North and South claimed a victory on March 9, 1862, many saw the outcome as a draw. Despite her wounded commander and damaged pilothouse,

When Union troops occupied Norfolk, Virginia, on May 10 1862, the CSS *Virginia* was unable to retreat further up the James River due to her deep draft. Nor was she seaworthy enough to escape into the Atlantic Ocean. Without a home port, the Confederate ironclad was ordered blown up to prevent capture. This task fell to Lieutenant Catesby ap Roger Jones, the last man to leave the vessel. In the early hours of May 11, the *Virginia* was run aground off Craney Island and set on fire. She exploded shortly after when the flames reached her magazine, sinking within minutes.

TOP
The power of the explosion is captured in hand-colored lithograph produced by Currier & Ives at New York in 1862.

BOTTOM
Settled on the riverbed, the wreck of the *Virginia*, plus that of the gunboat *Jamestown*, was photographed by a Northern photographer after the Confederate withdrawal. (Library of Congress - LC-USZC2-2252/LC-B8171-3350)

the *Monitor* had won a tactical victory. The Union ironclad had stopped the *Virginia* from destroying the *Minnesota*, which relieved Northern fears of a broken blockade and an attack on Washington, DC, via the Potomac River. However, the appearance of the *Virginia* in Hampton Roads posed a serious threat to Union war plans and affected the course of the Peninsula Campaign, due to begin on March 17, 1862. On March 9, McClellan wrote to General John Wool, commanding at Fortress Monroe, "The performances of the *Merrimack* place a new aspect upon everything. I may very probably change my old plan of campaign just on the eve of execution." The presence of the *Virginia* effectively closed off access to the James River. Moreover, instead of plying up the York River in support of McClellan's advance along the Peninsula, the Union navy was held in Hampton Roads to defend against the possibility of further sorties by the Confederate ironclad. Thus the *Virginia* virtually eliminated naval involvement in the Peninsula Campaign for several critical weeks, which seriously hampered the advance toward the Confederate capital at Richmond, preventing its capture and thereby prolonging the war by several years.

Despite their impact on naval history, the hulls of both the *Virginia* and *Monitor* were resting underwater by the end of the year. As the Confederates abandoned their positions in the Norfolk area, the Southern ironclad was threatened with the loss of her base. After a futile effort to lighten her draft sufficiently to be withdrawn up the James River toward Richmond, the Confederacy's formidable vessel was destroyed by her crew off Craney Island on May, 11, 1862, about 6 miles from where she had electrified the world a few months earlier. After further service in the James River in support of McClellan's Peninsular Campaign, the *Monitor* was ordered south for operations off Charleston, South Carolina, and foundered and sank during an Atlantic gale off Cape Hatteras, North Carolina, on December 30, 1862.

LATER UNION MONITOR-TYPE IRONCLADS

The success of the original *Monitor* produced a "monitor-mania" in the North, and the ship served as a prototype for the numerous other monitor-type vessels built during the Civil War. Of these, 21 seagoing vessels and seven river vessels were actually commissioned and saw war service. Developed in the aftermath of March 9, 1862, the *Passaic*-class monitor was an enlarged version of the original vessel. Commodore Joseph Smith, who had served on the original ironclad board, suggested alterations to the design of the ship. Ericsson responded with the plans for a new monitor, called USS *Passaic*. Externally, this new monitor varied from the original in a number of ways. The turret armor was increased from 8 to 11 inches thick; gun specifications required two XV-inch Dahlgren smoothbores; ventilation was improved; a permanent, armored smokestack was installed; and the pilothouse was relocated from the bow to a position surmounting the turret, where it would not obscure the field of fire of the vessel.

PASSAIC-CLASS MONITOR TECHNICAL SPECIFICATIONS

Dimensions: Length, 200 ft; Beam, 46 ft beam;
   Draft, 11 ft 6 in.
Designed speed: 7 knots
Tonnage: 1,335
Engines: Two Ericsson vibrating-lever engines
Boilers: Four

Crew size: 67/88
Armament: Designed to have two XV-inch Dahlgren
   smoothbores in turret, although only *Camanche*
   received this. *Lehigh* and *Patapsco* had one XV-inch
   Dahlgren and one 150-pdr Parrott rifle. The remainder
   had one XI-inch and one XV-inch Dahlgren each.

CANONICUS-CLASS MONITOR TECHNICAL SPECIFICATIONS

Dimensions: Length, 200 ft; Beam, 46 ft; Draft, 11 ft
   6 in. (except *Catawba* and *Oneota*: Length, 225 ft;
   Beam, 43 ft 3 in; *Tippecanoe*: Length, 224 ft;
   Beam, 43 ft; Draft, 11 ft 6 in; *Mahopac*,
   Manhattan, *Tecumseh*: Length, 223 ft; Beam, 43 ft
   4 in.)
Designed speed: 8 knots

Tonnage: 2,100
Engines: Two Ericsson vibrating-lever engines
Boilers: Two
Crew size: 85
Armament: All received two XV-inch Dahlgren
   smoothbores in turret, plus two 12-pdr Dahlgren
   howitzers on an iron field carriage

RIGHT
Published in *Harper's Weekly* on December 6, 1862, this engraving depicts USS *Passaic* "as she will appear at sea." This vessel was commissioned on November 25, 1862, and served in the North Atlantic Blockading Squadron taking part in the bombardment of the Fort McAllister, Georgia, on March 3, 1863, and the attack on the forts in Charleston harbor on April 7 of the same year. She was badly damaged during the latter action and had to return to New York for repairs. After further service, she was decommissioned in June 1865.

BELOW
Also included in the same journal was an impressive view of the interior of the *Passaic's* turret showing her XI and XV-inch Dahlgren smooth-bores. The different size of ordnance was necessary as the production of XV-inch guns initially could not keep up with demand. Note the round shot in the right hand foreground is in a hoisting sling ready to be loaded. The loading implements are stowed in the overhead, as in the *Monitor* turret. An arrow on the gun carriage indicates the turning direction of the compressor wheel. (Author's collection)

The nine other *Passaic*-class monitors were the USS *Camanche, Catskill, Lehigh, Montauk, Nahant, Nantucket, Patapsco, Sangamon,* and *Weehawken.* Costing about $400,000 each, these ships saw the most combat with Confederate forces and proved their worth far beyond their original contract price. Deployed to both the North and South Atlantic Blockading Squadrons, they took part in the bombardment of Confederate strongpoints at Fort McAllister, Georgia; Forts Wagner and Sumter, South Carolina; and New Smyrna, Florida, and between them captured nine blockade runners. One of the most celebrated vessels was the *Weehawken* which, with the *Nahant* in support, captured the Confederate ironclad *Atlanta* in June 1863 (see below). Later that year she went aground under fire at Charleston and sank with the loss of nearly half her crew. The *Patapsco* also sank after she hit a torpedo, or mine, in the Charleston River in January 1865. Seeing no Civil War service, the *Camanche* was shipped in parts to San Francisco aboard the *Aquila,* which sank at her pier in November 1863.

The second series of Ericsson monitors built during the Civil War was the *Canonicus*-class ship. Again an improvement in design based on experience gained from both the original *Monitor* and *Passaic,* the USS *Canonicus* was slightly longer but marginally narrower than the *Passaic.* Other improvements included thicker deck plating and improved ventilation. As these monitors had a similar external appearance, it was common practice to paint their turrets with unique patterns and colored stripes. The eight other vessels built in this class were the USS *Catawba, Mahopac, Manayunk, Manhattan, Oneota, Saugus, Tecumseh,* and *Tippecanoe.*

The *Canonicus* and *Saugus* served with the James River flotilla and later took part in operations against Fort Fisher, North Carolina, during December 1864 and January 1865. Dispatched to the Gulf Blockading Squadron, the *Manhattan* forced the surrender of the Confederate ironclad *Tennessee II* during the battle of Mobile Bay in August 1864. The *Tecumseh* sank during the same action (see below). The *Mahopac* assisted in the capture of Richmond in April 1865. The *Catawba, Manayunk, Oneota,* and *Tippecanoe* were launched and commissioned too late to see Civil War service.

A third class of monitor was developed during the Civil War, but this proved largely unsuccessful. This was a light draft vessel with single turret and turtle-back deck, commonly called the *Casco*-class, after the USS *Casco*. This type of vessel was developed to meet the needs of the Navy to operate along the shallow waters of the Mississippi River and it various tributaries. The other 19 *Casco*-class monitors were *Chimo, Cohoes, Etlah, Klamath, Koka, Modoc, Napa, Naubuc, Nausett, Shawnee, Shiloh, Squando, Suncook, Tunxis, Umpqua, Wassuc, Waxsaw, Yazoo,* and *Yuma.* The *Casco* monitors were to have a draft of only 6 feet and a freeboard of 15 inches, and were to be lightly

armored compared to their larger *Passaic* and *Canonicus* cousins. Although John Ericsson drew the original plans, they were altered by chief naval engineer Alban Stimers, who had served as adviser to the engineers aboard the original *Monitor.* The alterations made by Stimers included redesigning the ship to have a draft of only 4 feet, while increasing the armor on the decking and turret. Additional weight was also added by the placement of internal ballast tanks designed to be flooded to lower the silhouette of the vessel when going into battle. Furthermore, the *Casco*-class monitor had improved but heavier engines.

Unfortunately this additional weight sank the vessels into the water until they had less than 3 inches of freeboard, and subsequent leakage made them nearly useless. The only way to make them serviceable was to raise the deck by an additional 22 inches, which added 130 tons of displacement to these already overweight vessels. Only five *Casco*-class monitors, *Casco, Chimo, Modoc, Napa,* and *Naubuc,* were not altered in this manner. Minus the armored gun turret that was typical of monitor-type ironclads, two of these saw limited war service armed with spar torpedoes, or mines. The *Casco* served on the James River, while the *Chimo* was stationed at Hampton Roads and then off Point Lookout, North Carolina, in 1865.

The first double-turreted monitor, the USS *Onondaga,* was photographed in the James River, Virginia, circa 1864/65. Note the awnings over the turrets and deck in an attempt to reduce the impact of hot weather on the vessel and crew. A detachment of Marines man the row boat in the foreground. (Naval Historical Foundation photo NH 60210)

CASCO-CLASS MONITOR TECHNICAL SPECIFICATIONS

Dimensions: Length, 225 ft; Beam, 45 ft; Draft 9 ft 6 in.
Designed speed: 9 knots
Tonnage: 1,175 (except *Squando* 1,618 and *Nausett* 1,487)
Engines: Two inclined direct-acting engines
Crew size: 69

Armament: One XI-inch smoothbore, except *Cohoes, Shawnee, Squando, Wassuc:* two XI-inch smoothbores; *Tunxis:* one XI-inch smoothbore, one 150-pdr rifle; *Casco, Napa, Naubuc:* one XI-inch smoothbore, one spar torpedo; *Chimo,* one 150-pdr rifle, one spar torpedo; *Modoc,* one spar torpedo

Of the other Union seagoing monitors, the *Onondaga* was the first double-turreted monitor commissioned. The *Miantonomoh*-class of monitor was also twin-turreted and carried four XV-inch Dahlgren smoothbores. The four vessels commissioned in October 1864 consisted of the *Miantonomoh, Monadnock, Agamenticus,* and *Tonawanda.* Of these vessels, only the *Miantonomoh* and *Monadnock* saw a short period of Civil War service with the North Atlantic Squadron.

Other less successful monitors that failed to see battle included the four-(later three) turreted *Roanoke*; the *Dictator*, designed to be John Ericsson's ultimate expression of a true seagoing ironclad; and her sister ship, the *Puritan.* The largest and most expensive monitors were the four vessels of the *Kalamazoo*-class, after the USS *Kalamazoo.* Measuring 345 feet in length, they also were twin turreted, but were unfinished when the war ended.

Other Union river monitors included the USS *Ozark*, which combined a single turret with four guns in a casemate, and the *Neosho*-class designed by James B. Eads, of St. Louis, which included the *Neosho* and *Osage.* These were also single-turreted, with turtle-back casemate and very shallow 4-foot 6-inch draft. The *Milwaukee*-class double-turreted monitors, consisting of the *Chickasaw, Kickapoo, Milwaukee,* and *Winnebago*, were also designed by Eads, with one Ericsson turret and one Eads turret. The seven *City*-class casemated ironclads, made up of the *Cairo, Carondelet, Cincinnati, Louisville, Mound City, Pittsburg,* and *St. Louis*, were designed by Naval Constructor Samuel M. Pook. Known as "Pook Turtles," they had rectangular casemates similar to the Confederate design and a paddle wheel amidships near the stern.

OTHER CONFEDERATE CASEMATED IRONCLADS

Largely lacking the technology, the only attempt on the part of the Confederacy to build a monitor-type ironclad occurred at Columbus, Georgia, in early 1865. As planned, the vessel was to carry two 11in. smoothbore guns in a single turret, but the war ended before it could be launched. Thus, the South largely concentrated on the development of a series of casemated ironclads, all of which were based on the original *Virginia* prototype, for use on both river and sea. One exception was the "turtle-backed" *Manassas.* In September 1861, the towboat *Enoch Train* was converted into the ironclad ram *Manassas* at Algiers, Louisiana. A small vessel of only 387 tons with a convex, or turtle-back, hull plated with railroad iron, the *Manassas* carried only one smoothbore gun. Commanded by Commodore George N. Hollins, this vessel served in the Lower Mississippi River and was the first ironclad vessel in North America to see combat, predating both the *Virginia* and *Monitor.* On October 12, 1861, she attacked the Union blockading squadron at the Head of Passes, ramming the USS *Richmond* and being damaged in the process. She later engaged Union ships below New Orleans on April 24, 1862. Ramming several vessels, she ran aground and burned in the Mississippi River.

The *Arkansas*-class ironclads consisted of the *Arkansas* and the *Tennessee*, both of which were built at Memphis, Tennessee, by John T. Shirley & Co. The CSS *Arkansas*

was launched in April and commissioned in May 1862, while the *Tennessee* was never completed and burned on the stocks to prevent capture when Memphis fell on June 6, 1862. Measuring 175 feet in length, with a 35 foot beam and 11-foot 6-inch draft, the *Arkansas* had sloping casemated sides like the *Virginia* and was also armored with railroad iron placed over wood and compressed cotton. Under command of Lieutenant Isaac Newton Brown, she was towed to Yazoo City in an incomplete state with the capture of Memphis, and elements of the Confederate Army were enlisted to complete her construction. After five weeks she had been fully outfitted, except for the curved armor intended to surround her stern and pilothouse, and boiler plate was attached in a makeshift fashion to these areas. The *Arkansas* mounted ten heavy guns that consisted of two 8in. Columbiads in her bow ports and two 6.4 Brooke rifles in her stern ports. Her broadside battery was composed of two more Brooke rifles of the same caliber, plus two 8in. Dahlgrens and two 32-pdr smoothbores.

The *Arkansas* had a complement of 200, 60 of which were Missourian volunteers from the Confederate forces at Yazoo City who had never before served big guns or been aboard ship. Regardless, Brown steamed down the Yazoo River and engaged the Union ironclads *Carondelet*, *Tyler*, and *Queen of the West* on July 15, 1862. Hull-to-hull the *Arkansas* and the *Carondelet* pounded away at each other until the guns of the Confederate vessel devastated the Union ship and drove her aground. The *Tyler* also suffered heavy damage, while the *Queen of the West* withdrew to warn the Union ships moored above Vicksburg. The *Arkansas* next entered the Mississippi River and pounded her way through the rest of the combined Union fleets of Flag Officers Farragut and Davis, staying as close to the enemy vessels as possible in order to prevent being rammed and to cause as much confusion as possible. After half an hour, the battered Confederate ironclad passed the last enemy ship and limped to the dock at Vicksburg. Her crew suffered ten killed and 15 wounded, while the Union fleets lost 42 killed and 69 wounded.

Over the next month the *Arkansas* was attacked at her mooring several times, but in each instant the Union ships failed with heavy losses. As a result, the blockade of Vicksburg was lifted for four months, and the largest naval force ever assembled in the Western Hemisphere had been dispersed by a hastily built ironclad constructed with scrap metal and manned by a crew containing inexperienced volunteer soldiers. The

Arkansas was subsequently ordered downriver to support a land attack at Baton Rouge and broke down in sight of the Union fleet on August 6, 1862. Efforts were made by the crew to repair her defective engines as the enemy steamed toward them. Seeing that he could bring no guns to bear on the approaching ships, first officer Lieutenant Charles Read ordered most of his men ashore and, with the help of a few other officers, set fire to his vessel. Within minutes she exploded with colors still flying.

On May 9, 1861, the 1,006-ton *Atlanta* was launched at Savannah, Georgia, having been converted from the iron-hulled blockade runner *Fingal* by N. & A. Tift. Cut down to the waterline in similar fashion to the *Virginia*, the armored deck of the *Atlanta* projected 6 feet beyond the hull with a 4-inch thick casemate on top. Armed with two 7in. Brooke rifles and two 6.4in. Brooke rifles, and with a complement of 145 men, the *Atlanta* twice attempted to attack Union warships blockading the coast and rivers leading to Savannah. The first, in early 1863, was thwarted by obstructions blocking the route to the sea. In June 1863 she made her second attempt, targeting blockaders in Wassaw Sound. There, on June 17, she encountered the Union *Passaic*-class monitors *Nahant* and *Weehawken*. In a brief battle, the *Atlanta* went aground and was overwhelmed by the superior firepower of the *Weehawken*, which consisted of a XV-inch and an XI-inch Dahlgren, forcing her to surrender. The captured ironclad was taken into the Union navy as USS *Atlanta* and commissioned for service in February 1864.

The *Albemarle*-class ironclad consisted of the *Albemarle, Neuse,* and a third unnamed vessel. Each of these purpose-built vessels had an octagonal casemate on a flat hull, designed by Commander James W. Cooke, and built by Gilbert Elliot, who established a shipyard in a cornfield at Edwards Ferry on the Roanoke River in North Carolina. The CSS *Albemarle* was damaged during launch on July 1, 1863, and taken to Halifax, North Carolina, for completion. She attacked the Union squadron off Plymouth, North Carolina, sinking USS *Southfield* on April 19, 1864, and was damaged during a second attack on May 5 of the same year. She was finally sunk at her moorings in the Roanoke River by a Union spar torpedo boat on October 28, 1864. Raised by Union troops, she was taken to the Norfolk Navy Yard in April 1865.

The CSS *Neuse* was built by Elliot, Smith & Co. at Kinston on the Neuse River, North Carolina, and commissioned in April 1864. She ran aground off Kinston on her way to support Confederate operations at New Bern, NC during the next month. She was not refloated until June, by which time all operations in eastern North Carolina had ceased because army units had been recalled to Virginia to assist in the defense of Richmond. The *Neuse* remained inactive for a further ten months, when she was ordered to cover the evacuation of Kinston following the battle of Wyse Fork in March 1865. Her guns bombarded the Union Army while Confederate troops abandoned the town. Once the evacuation was complete, the *Neuse* was scuttled on March 9, 1865, to prevent capture.

By 1862, Chief Naval Constructor John Porter and the CS Navy Department had created a basic design for a new type of ironclad, of which six were made. Beginning with the *Richmond*, constructed at the Gosport Navy Yard, Virginia, Porter would maintain tight control over *Richmond*-class ironclad production for the remainder of the war. Sometimes referred to as *Virginia II* or the *Young Virginia,* the CSS *Richmond*

ALBEMARLE-CLASS IRONCLAD TECHNICAL SPECIFICATIONS

Dimensions: Length, 152 ft; Beam, 34 ft; Draft, 9 ft
Designed speed: 4 knots
Tonnage: 376
Engines: Two horizontal, noncondensing engines
  and two screws

Boilers: Two
Crew size: 50
Armament: Two 6.4in. Brooke rifles.

RICHMOND-CLASS IRONCLAD TECHNICAL SPECIFICATIONS

Dimensions: Length, 172 ft 6 in; Beam, 34 ft;
  Draft, 12 ft
Engines: One screw

Boilers: Two
Crew size: 180

was launched on May 6, 1862, and commissioned during the following July. Armed with one 7in. Brooke rifle, two 6.4in. Brooke rifles, one 10in. smoothbore, and a spar torpedo, the *Richmond* was assigned to the James River Squadron in defense of the Confederate capital. She took part in engagements at Dutch Gap on August 13, Fort Harrison on September 29–31, and Chapin's Bluff, October 22, 1864. Attacked while aground at Trent's Reach on January 23–24, 1865, she was scuttled to prevent capture prior to the fall of Richmond on April 3, 1865.

The CSS *Chicora* was built in Charleston, South Carolina, at the James Eason Shipyard and launched on August 23, 1862. Armed with four 6in. rifles and two 9in. smoothbores, she attacked the blockading fleet on January 31, 1863, in an unsuccessful attempt to recapture the British blockade runner *Princess Royal* – taken by the Union fleet two days earlier – with rifled guns, small arms, ammunition, and two powerful steam engines destined for new Confederate ironclads aboard. She subsequently took part in the defense of the Charleston forts on April 7 of that year and was eventually scuttled prior to the fall of Charleston on February 18, 1865. Another Charleston-built ironclad, the *Palmetto State,* was armed with ten 7in. rifles. She also took part in the attack on the blockaders in January 1863, on which occasion she rammed and badly damaged the USS *Mercedita.* The *Palmetto State* was scuttled on the same date as the *Chicora.*

The CSS *Savannah* was built at Willink's Ship Yard in Savannah, Georgia, and commissioned on June 30, 1863. Carrying two 7in. and two 6.4in. rifles, she served in defense of her namesake city until scuttled prior to capture on December 21, 1864. Built at Berry and Brothers Ship Yard, on Eagles Island, at Wilmington, North Carolina, the CSS *North Carolina* was clad with railroad iron like the *Virginia*, and had two gun ports on each of her four sides. However, she carried only seven 8in. guns, six of which could be moved from one port to another. The seventh piece was a pivot gun on her bow. Also, like the *Virginia*, this ironclad had defective engines, confiscated from the US tug *Uncle Ben*, which affected her service. The *North Carolina* took part in only one partially successful action against the Union blockading fleet, on May 6, 1864, following which she was used as a guard vessel commanding the entrance to the Cape Fear River.

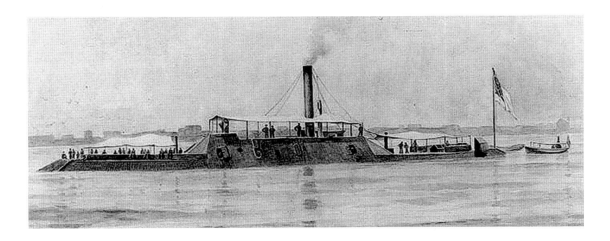

Also built in North Carolina at the shipyard of J. L. Cassidy & Sons in Wilmington was the CSS *Raleigh*, commissioned on April 30, 1864, under the command of Lieutenant J. Pembroke Jones, CSN. Taking part in the defense of Wilmington, the *Raleigh* engaged Union blockading vessels with her four 6in. rifles off New Inlet on May 6, 1864, but went aground and was wrecked on Wilmington Bar the next day.

The CSS *Louisiana* was built at New Orleans at the Murray Ship Yard and launched on February 6, 1862. A 1,400-ton vessel, she was slightly longer than the *Virginia*, measured 264 feet in length with a 62-foot beam. She was powered by engines taken from the steamer *Ingomar*, which supplied the motive force for two paddle wheels set in a center well one behind the other, plus twin rudders. Protected by 4-inch-thick iron plating, she carried 16 guns consisting of two 7in. rifles, three 9in. and four 8in. rifles, and seven 32-pdr. Towed while incomplete to Fort St Philip below New Orleans on April 20, 1862, the *Louisiana* was used as a floating battery and blown up to prevent capture when the Union fleet forced the mouth of the Mississippi River several days later.

Another type of vessel developed by CS Naval Constructor John Porter, the *Columbia*-class ironclad had a shorter casemate to cope with an increasing shortage of metal for plating in the South. Constructed by Jones & Eason at Charleston, South Carolina, the CSS *Columbia* was launched in March 1864 and commissioned later that year. Protected by 6-inch-thick plate iron, her 189-foot long casemate contained six guns. Sooner after launch, this vessel ran into a sunken wreck near Fort Moultrie on January 12, 1865. She was later salvaged by the US Navy. A modified *Columbia*-class vessel, the CSS *Tennessee II* was the only Confederate ironclad that actually did battle with a *Canonicus*-class monitor. A 1,273-ton vessel, she was 209 feet in length with a 189-foot long casemate, and had a 48-foot beam and 14-foot draft. She was laid down at Selma, Alabama, in October 1862 and finally commissioned on February 16, 1864. Her armament consisted of two 7in. and four 6.4in. Brooke rifles protected by a 189-foot long casemate covered with 6-inch-thick iron plating with a wood backing.

Serving as the flagship for Admiral Franklin Buchanan, commander of CSS *Virginia* in March 1862, the *Tennessee II*, aided by the gunboats *Morgan*, *Gaines*, and

A modified *Columbia*-class vessel with a shortened casemate, the CSS *Tennessee II* was the only Confederate ironclad to encounter *Canonicus*-class monitors. (Courtesy of the US Navy Art Collection, Washington D.C.)

OVERLEAF
During an attempt to attack the Union blockading fleet in Wassaw Sound off the Georgia coast on June 17, 1863, the Confederate casemated ironclad CSS *Atlanta* ran aground and was pounded into submission by the greater fire-power of the XV-inch Dahlgrens aboard the Passaic-class monitor USS *Weehawken*.

Selma, confronted the Union fleet under Rear Admiral Farragut during the battle of Mobile Bay on August 5, 1864. As the enemy ships approached, exchanging fire with Fort Morgan, Buchanan's small flotilla attempted to meet them with a head-on. Meanwhile, the Union *Canonicus*-class monitor *Tecumseh* veered off course and struck a mine and sank, temporarily throwing the attacking column into confusion. Lashed securely in the rigging of his flagship, Farragut ordered the USS *Hartford* to take the lead using the immortal words, "Damn the torpedoes! Full steam ahead!" He drove off the Confederate gunboats, but *Tennessee II* remained within range, firing on the Union vessels as they passed, doing considerable damage to the last in line, the USS *Oneida*.

With the enemy inside the bay, Buchanan steamed toward them, being rammed by three separate vessels and subjected to a terrific cannonade from the *Hartford*. The monitors *Chickasaw* and *Manhattan* then engaged her at close range with their heavy guns, while other Union ships fired from a distance. The Confederate ironclad's smokestack and most other external fittings were shot away. Her gun port shutter chains were cut, closing the ports and rendering her guns useless. Her exposed steering chains were severed, leaving her unmanageable. The *Manhattan* blew a hole in her casemate with her massive 15in. gun. The twin-turreted *Milwaukee*-class monitor *Chickasaw* stationed herself off the beleaguered ship's stern, firing her XI-inch guns and seriously weakening the after-end of *Tennessee II*'s casemate.

With his flagship unable to fire her guns, steam, or steer, and with the collapse of the casemate seemingly imminent, the wounded Confederate Admiral Buchanan authorized surrender, and Commander James D. Johnston poked a white flag through the top of the casemate. Although firing soon ceased, the USS *Ossipee,* coming on fast in another ramming attempt, was unable to stop in time, and struck a postsurrender blow. Union navy officers soon took possession of the battered *Tennessee II*, effectively concluding the battle of Mobile Bay, thus ending one of the last major attempts by a Confederate ironclad to achieve a victory at sea.

Other Confederate casemated ironclads engaged in river combat toward the end of the war were the *Fredericksburg,* which saw action at Trent's Reach on the James River on June 21, 1864, and the *Virginia II*, which was involved in the same action, plus that at Dutch Gap on August 13 and October 22, 1864, and a second encounter at Trent's Reach on January 23–24, 1865. Confederate ironclads laid down but not launched or commissioned included the *Huntsville*-class, consisting of the *Huntsville* and *Tuscaloosa*, neither of which saw service and were sunk as block ships in the Mobile River on April 12, 1865; the *Columbia*-class *Jackson* (also known as the *Muscogee*), which was destroyed by Union cavalry before completion at Confederate States Yard, Columbus, Georgia, on April 17, 1864; the *Milledge*-class ironclads, all four of which were destroyed on the stocks to prevent capture in December 1864; and the *Nashville*, which was surrendered incomplete in the Tombigbee River on May 10, 1865. The *Columbia*-class *Texas* was the last ironclad the Confederacy tried to build. Laid down in Richmond and launched in January 1865, she remained unfinished when the Richmond Navy Yard fell to Union forces.

AFTERMATH

In the years following the Civil War, many of the monitors of the US Navy were sold at bargain prices as Congress failed to recognize the need to maintain a substantial presence at sea. The *Canonicus*-class vessels *Catawba* and *Oneota* were sold to Peru in 1868. *Casco*-class monitors such as the *Chimo, Cohoes, Etlah, Klamath, Modoc,* and *Shiloh* were sold for private use, or were broken up in 1874. The legislators of the time failed to acknowledge or appreciate the fact that the United States had become a world naval power and had clearly demonstrated that fact on a March day at Hampton Roads during 1862. The postwar American mood had more to do with unfinished business than maintaining and improving a strong navy. The American West had to be tamed and carved up into proper territories and then transformed into states. The policies of reconstruction and retribution in the Southern States had to be pursued. The five years after the war witnessed much more effort toward creating and passing three Constitutional amendments than worrying about a fleet.

In 1873 the Spanish Navy stopped the *Virginius*, a Cuba-bound American registered ship, and removed her captain, Joseph Fry, an ex-Confederate naval officer, and 45 men of the 170 people aboard. Spanish suspicions that the vessel was attempting to aid the Cuban revolutionary movement proved well founded, and a Spanish firing squad delivered speedy punishment. The American nation was incensed, but only a small battle-ready fleet was available to meet the Spanish on the high seas or prevent a Spanish fleet from entering US waters. Most importantly, there were no ironclads available to go to sea or protect the American coastline.

The *Virginius* affair goaded Congress into appropriating funds to finish off or update the remaining old monitors, and Secretary of the Navy George M. Robeson was authorized to use about $900,000 for "reconstruction of the iron fleet." The five monitors selected were the still incomplete single-turreted *Puritan* and four

The *Passaic*-class USS *Jason* (ex-*Sangamon*) was photographed on May 27 1898, probably at the New York Navy Yard, after she had been recommissioned for coastal defense service during the Spanish-American War. (Naval Historical Foundation photo NH 44266)

Miantonomoah-class monitors. Their old hulls were dismantled and new vessels begun, but they retained their old names since Congress had only authorized reconstruction. However, work on these monitors was suspended in 1876, as Congress once again failed to see the need for a major presence at sea.

As late as 1888 the US Navy still mainly consisted of wooden cruising ships and smaller gunboats carrying full sail-rig with auxiliary steam power. Its role was purely to "show the flag" around the world and protect American commercial interests. Except for coastal trade, the US merchant marine had been in a state of continual decline since the Civil War when foreign commercial interests had entrusted their goods on a long term basis to carriers of other nations who would not fall prey to the high seas raiders of the Confederacy.

But the likes of Rear Admirals Alfred Thayer Mahan, Stephen B. Luce, and William Sampson were biding their time in the study and development of a new American steel navy. Arising from the naval ashes of the early 1890s, a new fleet would emerge in response to the sinking of the USS *Maine* in Havana Harbor on February 15, 1898, which the US controversially blamed on Spain. Included in the American naval preparations for an offensive against the Spanish colonial empire in the Caribbean and Pacific were the rusty old *Passaic*-class monitors *Catskill* (renamed *Goliath*) *Lehigh*, *Nahant*, *Passaic*, and *Sangamon*, which were used for patrol duty in New England waters, thereby releasing more modern ships for active fighting. But the earlier achievement of these iron monsters with massive guns in revolving turrets lived on in the annals of history and would inspire a new generation of naval architects who would produce steel battleships for a modern navy to take the United States into the 20th century as a world power.

BIBLIOGRAPHY AND FURTHER READING

During the battle of Mobile Bay, on August 5, 1864, the CSS *Tennessee* served as the flagship of Admiral Franklin Buchanan, previous commander of CSS *Virginia*, and was bombarded into submission by the *Chickasaw* and *Manhattan,* plus the *Milwaukee*-class double-turreted *Chickasaw*. In this painting by Xanthus Smith, the *Tennessee II* and *Chickasaw* are in the foreground, the USS *Hartford*, flagship of Rear Admiral David G. Farragut, is right center, and the *Winnebago* is in the left distance. (Courtesy of the U.S. Naval Academy Museum, Annapolis, Maryland)

BOOKS

Baxter, James Phinney, III, *The Introduction of the Ironclad*, Harvard University Press, Cambridge, MA (1933)

Daly, Robert W., *How the Merrimac Won: The Strategic Story of CSS Virginia*, Thomas Y. Crowell, New York (1957)

———— (ed.), *Aboard the U.S.S. Monitor: 1862 – The Letters of Acting Paymaster*

William Frederick Keeler, U.S. Navy to his Wife, Anna, United States Naval Institute Press, Annapolis, MD (1964)

Donnelly, Ralph W., *Service Records of Confederate Enlisted Marines,* Owen G. Dunn Co., New Bern, NC (1979)

————, *The Confederate States Marine Corps,* White Mane Publishing Company, Shippenburg, PA (1989)

Flanders, Alan B., *The Merrimac: The Story of the Conversion of the U.S.S. Merrimac into the Confederate Ironclad Warship C.S.S. Virginia,* Navy Shipyard Museum, Portsmouth, VA (1982)

————, *John L. Porter, Naval Constructor of Destiny,* Brandylane Publishers, White Stone, VA (2000)

Harlowe, Jerry, *Monitors: The Men, Machines and Mystique,* Thomas Publications, Gettysburg, PA (2001)

Herbert, H. A. (director), *Official Records of the Union and Confederate Navies in the War of the Rebellion,* 31 volumes, Government Printing Office, Washington, DC (1895–1929)

Hewett, Janet B., Noah Andre Trudeau, and Bryce A. Suderow (editors), *Supplement to the Official Records of the Union and Confederate Armies,* 100 volumes, Broadfoot Publishers, Wilmington, NC (1994–2001)

Jack, Eugenius A., *Memoirs of E. A. Jack; Steam Engineer, C.S.S. Virginia,* Alan B. Flanders and Neale O. Westfall (editors), Brandylane Publishers, White Stone, VA (1998)

Konstam, Angus, *Hampton Roads 1862,* Osprey Publishing, Oxford (2002)

————, *Duel of the Ironclad: USS Monitor & CSS Virginia at Hampton Roads 1862,* Osprey Publishing, Oxford (2003)

Mindell, David A., *War, Technology, and Experience Aboard the USS Monitor,* John Hopkins University Library, Baltimore, MD (2000)

Ordnance Instructions for the United States Navy, Government Printing Office, Washington, DC (1866)

Peck, Taylor, *Round-shot to Rockets: A History of the Washington Navy Yard and U.S. Naval Gun Factory,* United States Naval Institute, Annapolis, MD (1949)

Quarstein, John V., *C.S.S. Virginia: Mistress of Hampton Roads,* H. E. Howard, Inc., Appomattox, VA (2000)

Scott, Robert R. (compiler), *The War of the Rebellion: A Compilation of the Official Records of the Union and Confederate Armies,* 120 volumes, Government Printing Office, Washington, DC (1880–1901)

Sharf, J. Thomas, *History of the Confederate States Navy,* Rogers and Sherwood, New York (1887)

Silverstone, Paul H., *Warships of the Civil War Navies,* Naval Institute Press, Annapolis, MD (1989)

Still, William N., Jr., *Iron Afloat: The Story of the Confederate Armourclad* Vanderbilt University Press, Nashville, TN (1971)

Tucker, Spencer, *Arming the Fleet: US Navy Ordnance in the Muzzle-Loading Era,* Naval Institute Press, Annapolis, MD (1989)

ARTICLES

Eggleston, John R., "Captain Eggleston's Narrative of the Battle of the Merrimac," *Southern Historical Society Papers,* Vol. 41 (1916), Richmond, VA, pp. 166–178

Greene, S. Dana, "In the 'Monitor' Turret," *Battles & Leaders of the Civil War*, Vol. 1 (1956), Thomas Yoseloff, New York, pp. 719–729

"Interesting Facts about the Merrimac," *The Scientific American,* New Series, Vol. VI, No. 23 (June 7, 1862), p. 355

Phillips, Dinwiddie B., "The Career of the Merrimac," *The Southern Bivouac,* New Series 2, No. 10 (March 1887), pp. 598–608

Ramsay, Henry Ashton, "The Most Famous of Sea Duels, The Story of the Merrimac's Engagement with the Monitor, and the Events That Preceded and Followed The Fight, Told by a Survivor," *Harper's Weekly* (February 10, 1912), pp. 11–12

"The Ram Merrimac," *Southern Historical Society Papers*, Vol. 20 (January 1892), pp. 3–34.

Wood, John Taylor, "The First Fight of the Ironclads; March 9, 1862," *Battles and Leaders of the Civil War*, Vol. 1 (1956) Thomas Yoseloff, New York, pp. 699–711

In this moment of relaxation aboard USS *Catskill,* Lieutenant Commander Edward Barrett is seated in front of the pilothouse which surmounted the turret of the *Passaic*-class monitors. The 11in. and 15in. Dahlgrens peer through her gun ports, while her two 12-lb brass boat guns stand at the ready either side. Note how the muzzle of the 15in. gun remains within the turret, while the 11in. clears the gun port. (Library of Congress LC-B8171-3412)

NEWSPAPERS

"Burning of the Navy-yard!" *The Richmond (Virginia) Daily Dispatch,* April 23, 1861

"Steel-clad Ships," *The New York Times*, August 8, 1861

"The Great Naval Victory," *The Richmond (Virginia) Daily Dispatch,* March 11, 1862

"The Iron-Clad Steamer 'Virginia,'" *The Richmond (Virginia) Daily Dispatch* March 19, 1862

"The Steam Frigate Merrimac," *Daily Lynchburg Virginian*, September 12, 1861

"The Virginia," *Daily Richmond Enquirer*, April 3, 1862

The (Virginia) Norfolk, March 10, 1862

"War Movements," *The Richmond (Virginia) Daily Dispatch,* June 29, 1861

INDEX